Microeconomics for **A Level Year 1** and **AS**

Andrew Threadgould
Staff Tutor, Dulwich College

and **Amy Meachen**

For Charlotte and James Meachen

and

Jacob, Phoebe and Clara Threadgould

© Anforme Ltd 2015
ISBN 978-1-78014-009-4
Images supplied by Shutterstock.com

Anforme Ltd, Stocksfield Hall, Stocksfield, Northumberland NE43 7TN.

Typeset by George Wishart & Associates, Whitley Bay.
Printed by Potts Print (UK) Ltd.

Contents

Part One   **Markets**

Chapter 1   **The Economic Problem** 1

Chapter 2   **The Theory of Demand** 9

Chapter 3   **The Theory of Supply** 12

Chapter 4   **Markets and Equilibrium** 16

Chapter 5   **Elasticity** 23

Chapter 6   **Interrelated Markets and Markets in Action** 33

Part Two   **Markets and Government Failure**

Chapter 7   **Introduction to Market Failure** 46

Chapter 8   **Monopoly Power and Competition** 49

Chapter 9   **Externalities** 58

Chapter 10   **Public, Merit and Demerit Goods** 67

Chapter 11   **Factor Immobility and Inequality** 75

Chapter 12   **Government Policy and Government Failure** 80

              Index 88

Part One: Markets

Chapter 1
The Economic Problem

Introduction to Microeconomics

Microeconomics examines the decisions made by individual economic agents such as consumers, workers and firms. As a social science, economics takes a logical, model-building approach to the behaviour of people and organisations. Microeconomics can be separated into two broad areas: **markets** and **market failure**. The first six chapters of this book examine markets and their importance at the heart of economic theory; the final six chapters explore the potential problems of leaving all economic decisions to market forces.

Resources and scarcity

An economy converts inputs, or resources (factors of production), into output (goods and services).

There are four factors of production: land, labour, capital and entrepreneurship. Land includes physical space for factories and roads as well as raw materials such as oil, copper, fertile soil and water. Labour, also called human capital, is the workforce of an economy. Capital, or physical capital, is the sum of buildings (such as factories and offices), machinery, vehicles and computers used by workers to help them produce output. Entrepreneurship is managerial ability: the drawing together of land, labour and capital into the productive process.

Factors of production earn payments as shown in Table 1.1.

Table 1.1 Payments for factors of production

Land	–	Rent
Labour	–	Wages
Capital	–	Interest
Entrepreneurship	–	Profit

Financial capital, or money, is sometimes suggested by students as the most important factor of production. In fact, money is simply a means of measuring and comparing the value of both resources and output, and is not a factor of production in its own right.

Resources are **scarce**, or **limited**. There is only a fixed amount of land, people, machinery and managerial expertise at any point in time, and even though one economy may increase their resource stock – by developing their own factors, or stealing someone else's (historically, most wars have been fought over territory, i.e. land, or the resources it holds, e.g. oil) – the resources available will always be outstripped by the wants and needs of the population.

It is important to consider the sustainability of resources and to examine the implications of economic activity for the environment.

Resources can be divided into renewable and non-renewables.

Non-renewable resources include fossil fuels, wood, and fish stocks; there is a fixed supply of these resources and, once used up, there will be no more available. Resource use which has this impact is regarded as *unsustainable*.

Renewable resources include wind and tidal power; use of these resources does not reduce the amount available in the future, thus their use is regarded as *sustainable*.

Some non-renewable resources can be replenished if used in a sustainable way, for example if the use of trees is balanced with replanting programmes, or if fishing is limited to a level which allows for sufficient breeding to maintain a stable fish population.

Sustainable economic activity can be seen as limiting: it reduces production and consumption in the short-run. However, unsustainable economic activity will have an even larger impact longer-term in reducing options for future generations. This is known as *intergenerational inequality*, where people currently enjoy a standard of living which could threaten the wellbeing of future generations.

Wants and needs

Wants and needs are **unlimited**. **Needs** are those things necessary for human survival: food, water, warmth, shelter and clothing. **Wants** are items which are not strictly needed but, without which, human existence would be less satisfying. In modern economies, it is usual for people to refer to a want as a need, for example, "I need a new phone"!

Economists call people consumers and the act of consumption is the process of using a good or service, whether it is an apple, an iPod or a train journey. Some goods and services are durable, i.e. consumed over a period of time (a fridge, a travelcard) and others are non-durable, i.e. consumed at a point in time (a sandwich, a taxi ride).

If you were given £10 to spend this weekend, you could find something to spend it on. The same would apply to £100, £1000, or even £1m. People generally prefer more to less, and whether we are living at the most basic level of subsistence or in an advanced economy in the 21st Century, we can always find something extra we would like to consume.

This means that consumers will always be left unsatisfied. The resources simply do not exist to produce the goods and services needed to give everybody what they want (the debate regarding the world's capacity to give everyone on it what they *need* is a separate, if important issue) and thus a choice must be made. This necessary, if difficult, choice has earned economics the title of 'the dismal science' in some quarters!

Table 1.2

The Basic Economic Problem is that resources are finite, but wants and needs are infinite

Therefore we must choose **what** to produce, **how** to produce it, and **who** to produce it for

The basic economic problem exists on an individual level as most of us survive on a specified or limited income. Even the most indulged of your classmates will be given only a certain amount of money or allowance to spend, and even the richest people in an economy must decide what they can – and cannot – afford.

Opportunity cost

Whenever a choice is made, another opportunity is foregone. Your decision to study Economics at AS level means that you cannot study French, Politics, Biology or whatever your other fourth choice would have been. Economists call this **opportunity cost**: the benefits foregone of the next best alternative. If you were torn between studying Economics and Chemistry, for example, then the opportunity cost of opting for Economics is all the pleasure and knowledge you would have derived from choosing AS Chemistry.

The concept of opportunity cost can be applied to the decisions made by all economic agents. Households allocate limited income between the consumption of different goods and services, and also consider when to use their time for leisure, for study or for work. Firms must decide how best to use their space, capital and financial budgets and the goodwill of their staff. Governments must set priorities for spending and legislation.

Figure 1.1: Production possibility frontier

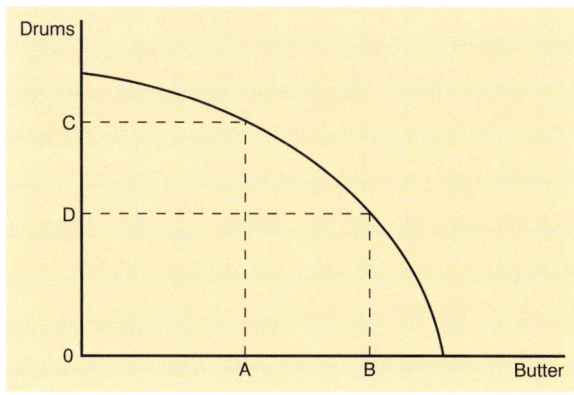

Figure 1.2: Changes in the trade-off between two goods

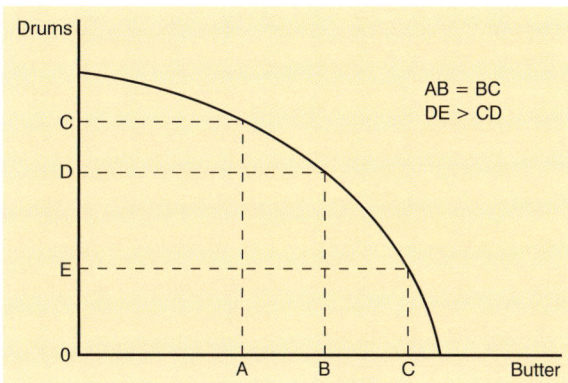

Opportunity cost can be illustrated on a production possibility frontier or PPF (also called a production possibility curve, production possibility boundary, production possibility diagram or even sometimes a transformation curve).

The PPF in Figure 1.1 shows the different possible maximum combinations of output of two goods, butter and drums. The PPF is drawn for a fixed number of inputs, or resources.

An increase in production of butter from A to B implies that the maximum output of drums falls from C to D. Thus the opportunity cost of AB more butter is CD fewer drums.

The PPF is usually drawn as concave to the origin. As the economy produces higher levels of butter, therefore, the opportunity cost in terms of drums rises. This is illustrated on Figure 1.2 where increases in butter of AB and BC cause different responses in terms of the number of drums foregone; although AB and BC are identical changes, CD is smaller than DE.

This shape is explained by changes in the trade-off between two goods as an economy specialises production in one industry. Factors of production in an economy are better suited to one industry than another, and thus when the output of butter approaches its maximum the extra land, labour and capital used will be taken from the drum industry. These resources are less effective (economists use the terms

As an economy produces higher levels of butter the opportunity cost in terms of drums rises.

Figure 1.3: Unemployment and the PPF

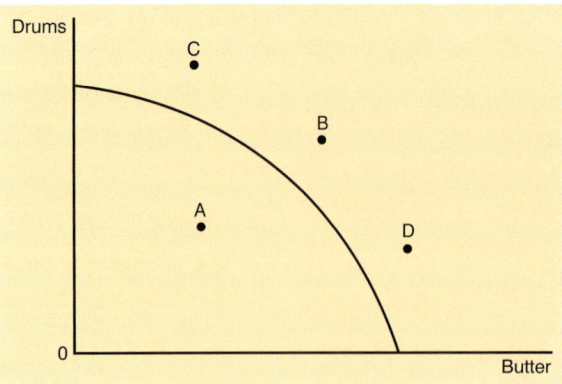

Figure 1.4: Negative growth and the PPF

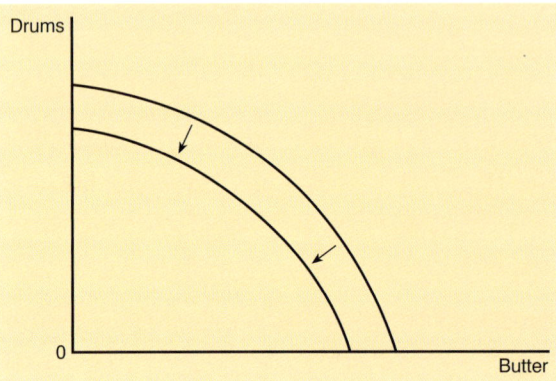

Figure 1.5: Growth and the PPF

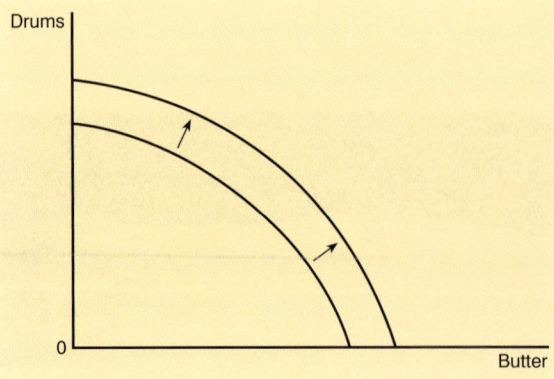

productive or efficient in this context) at producing butter than they were at making drums, and so the increase in butter production is lower than the fall in drums. Thus as the output of a good approaches its maximum level, the opportunity cost of any extra output will increase.

Productivity measures output relative to inputs. Labour productivity, for example, measures output per worker. Productivity increases when output rises more rapidly than input.

An economy may be operating within the PPF if there are unemployed resources. This is shown in Figure 1.3. All points inside the PPF represent output combinations which are possible, or attainable given the current levels of factors of production. All points outside the PPF are unobtainable, for example points B, C and D on Figure 1.3. In order for these combinations of output to be produced, there must be an increase in the quantity and/or the quality of factors of production.

All combinations of output on the PPF are regarded as productively efficient as they show that all resources are being used fully. This should be distinguished from negative growth in the economy, which may result from a war or a natural disaster which destroys factors of production. Figure 1.4 shows how this would result in a shift inwards of the PPF and could also be caused by a fall in the size of the population.

An increase in the quantity and/or quality of factors of production will shift the PPF outwards, as shown in Figure 1.5. Technological improvements may be an important factor in shifting out the PPF.

Value judgements

The PPF shows all possible combinations of output in an economy, but the decision about which combination is most appropriate requires an opinion, or a subjective value judgement. Consider the following statements:

1. Governments should spend more on healthcare than defence
2. Greater government involvement in our lives is a bad thing
3. Alcohol consumption in the UK is too high
4. Greater spending on healthcare will increase life expectancy

The first three statements are different from the fourth. The first three represent *value judgements* or *normative statements* and represent an opinion rather than a fact.

The final statement, on the other hand, can be found to be true or false if empirically tested. A study could be undertaken over time to isolate the impact of healthcare spending on life expectancy and it will be found to be a determining factor or not. Statements such as these are called positive statements. (This is explored in more detail below in the section Economics as a social science.) Note that a positive statement is not necessarily true – but it can be tested for truth. For example, "My chair is made of cheese" is likely to be false, but it is a positive statement because it can be proved to be false.

Economics students often ask what the 'right' policy is for a particular circumstance, such as what changes to tax or government spending is required, or which goods should be banned or even made freely available. These decisions should be made with reference to objective, positive economic analysis, but invariably there will also be the need to make a value judgement.

For example, which is most important: spending on care for the elderly, or hospital facilities for babies? Is education a greater priority than banking? The government's resources are limited, but the wants and needs – and expectations – of the electorate are infinite!

Economics can help a government to make the best decisions, but political and moral factors must also be considered.

The model of the PPF explained above gives economists the possible maximum output combinations available for the given level of resources. Any point on the PPF shows **productive efficiency**. However, the actual point they should choose is open to debate. Different combinations of output levels require different allocations of resources, and only by finding out what the economy wants can the 'best' point be calculated. This is called **allocative efficiency** and it will be achieved at the output combination where social welfare is maximised.

Goods and services

Goods are tangible or physical products, whereas services are intangible: acts done to or for a person. To avoid writing 'goods and services' every time, the term **goods** usually refers to both goods and services.

Economists distinguish between economic goods and free goods. **Economic goods** incur an opportunity cost whereas free goods do not. **Free goods** include fresh air and by-products such as pollution (this is sometimes referred to as a 'bad'). In reality, most goods are economic goods in that the resources used to produce them could have been used to produce something else. Note that a free good does not include a free gift or offer (for example a free DVD given away in a Sunday newspaper). These DVDs, although 'free' to the reader, do incur an opportunity cost in that the factors of production used to make them could have been used to make an alternative good. This distinction is the theory behind the expression, 'there is no such thing as a free lunch'.

Economic agents

Traditional economic theory makes the assumption that most of us are **rational** and pursue **maximising behaviour**. Economic agents are the decision-makers in an economy, and they include consumers, workers, firms and governments.

Consumers aim to **maximise utility**, the name economists use for pleasure or happiness. Thus every decision we make about what to spend our limited budget on incurs an opportunity cost. The £6 cinema ticket means we cannot afford a novel or a pizza or a new scarf. Assuming consumers act rationally, we spend the £6 on the good which will give us the most satisfaction. If this is the cinema ticket, its opportunity cost is the pleasure we would have gained from the next best alternative, or our second choice – say, the pizza.

Microeconomics for A Level Year 1 and AS

Workers aim to maximise **wages and other benefits**. A rational worker chooses to work in the industry where they are rewarded the most for their skills, qualifications and experience. Note that this will include both financial and non-financial rewards in both the short-run and long-run. Relatively low paid jobs may have significant advantages such as generous pension schemes, family-friendly working hours or long holidays.

Workers aim to maximise wages and other benefits.

Firms aim to **maximise profits**. Profit is the reward to entrepreneurs or managers for risk-taking. Starting a business carries considerable risk in terms of both money and time and most new firms fail within the first two years. Profit is the compensation from this, and capitalist or market economies are based on the concept that the better a good satisfies its consumers' wants and needs, the higher the potential for profit will be.

Governments aim to **maximise social welfare**. This assumption is debatable and is questioned at length in Chapter 12 when we examine Public Choice Theory.

Economics as a social science

Economics is a **social science** in that it seeks to explain human behaviour through models. An economic model, or theory, seeks to explain how people will generally behave in certain circumstances. These models can then be used to predict patterns of future behaviour by considering how one 'variable' (say, a government policy, or a change in perception) can influence another variable (such as whether a person smokes or not, or the spending level of a consumer).

An important character in economics is the 'rational economic person'. When we behave **rationally**, we are taking account of all available information and making a decision accordingly. This assumption of 'rationality' can contradict our everyday experiences, where we and the people we know actually appear to behave **irrationally**, choosing courses of action which create more harm than good.

The debate over rationality is one of the ideas explored by **behavioural economics**, a subject which uses both economics and psychology to try to explain human actions.

It is important to remember that social sciences differ from natural sciences (physical sciences such as physics, chemistry, or astronomy; and life sciences, such as biology). Most sciences which you have studied before will have allowed for laboratory testing. Laboratory conditions allow scientists to isolate the variables they are investigating and test for the strength of connection between the change and the impact of the experiment. Social sciences are different: economic agents such as households and firms make decisions against the backdrop of constant changes in mood, perception and finances. This inability of economists to emulate the laboratory conditions used in the natural sciences leads to the need to make assumptions about the background 'noise' in economic theory. The term 'ceteris paribus' is an important assumption in economics: it translates roughly as "all other things being equal". This allows economists to generalise but can also weaken the strength of economic predictions. If everything else is not actually equal, the impact of one change on another can change in different circumstances, sometimes quite dramatically.

Modern economists have been forced to consider how perfectly theory can explain the real world in light of recent events, from the failure of financial economists to predict the macroeconomic chaos of the 2007 Credit Crisis and ensuing recession of the late 2000s, to individual decisions which firms take to improve their profitability which can actually have the opposite effect, or lead to bankruptcy.

Specialisation and the division of labour

If we took a trip back in time to the prehistoric age we would see a very primitive economy at work. Yet even hunter-gatherer societies understood the importance of a central economic idea: specialisation.

Some people are better at some things than others. If your Economics teacher swapped places with your French teacher for a week, the quality of your lessons in both subjects would (except in rare circumstances) deteriorate considerably. This illustrates the power of specialisation. As economies develop, the level of specialisation tends to increase. Adam Smith, the father of modern economics, identified the importance of specialisation in his 1776 book, *The Wealth of Nations*, in which he referred to it as the **division of labour**.

Specialisation allows workers to improve their efficiency and productivity as they perform a relatively small number of tasks over and over again. As well as your Economics teacher being better at teaching about PPFs than teaching irregular French verbs, each year they teach the same topics they will find better ways of explaining it to their students.

Specialisation allows economic agents to produce a surplus: more of a good or service than they need. They then trade 'these' surpluses with other economic agents. For example, your Economics teacher produces more Economics lessons than their household needs, but the lessons (or at least the labour required to produce them) are sold in the labour market and the payments for this (your teacher's **wage**) can be used to buy other goods and services, such as books, holidays, clothes and wine.

Specialisation is the foundation of economic growth and prosperity in any economic system and the concept of **efficiency**, or **productivity**, is key. **Productivity** measures the relationship between output and input.

The productivity of a student preparing for a test could be measured by the improvement in their result in relation to the time and effort they spend revising. If two students spend an hour preparing for a test, the most productive student will see their score increase the most, compared to if they did not revise at all.

Similarly, more productive economies produce more goods and services per factor of production. **Labour productivity** measures the output per worker (in a firm, an industry, a region, or a whole economy) over a given period of time. Generally, higher levels of specialisation increase productivity, but specialisation can also create problems for an economy.

Advantages of specialisation	Disadvantages of specialisation
Factors of production are put to their most productive use, and total output in the economy therefore rises.	Changes in consumer demand may leave firms (and, in highly specialised economies) the whole economy with unwanted output and thus unprofitable capital and labour.
Over time, labour becomes more experienced and workers skills develop, further increasing productivity, output and therefore prosperity.	Structural unemployment may occur: this is where a worker has skills which are only suited to declining industries; without retraining, they may lack the skills to find a new job in a growing industry.
Firms see it is possible to invest in capital goods which may only be relevant to their own industry, further increasing labour productivity.	Countries which specialise in a single, lucrative industry (such as oil, or diamonds) often have strong currencies which make other export industries unprofitable, and leaves the economy vulnerable ('Dutch Disease').

Specialisation therefore requires a *system of exchange*. This exchange may be organised by the government (Socialism, or Communism) but more usually market forces are used to allocate factors of production to the industries where they will be most highly valued. Chapters 2, 3 and 4 explain this in detail to build a model of market behaviour using the theories of demand and supply.

Summary questions

1. What is an economy? What does it do?
2. Explain the four factors of production, give an example of each and state the payment to the factor.
3. What is the difference between a good and a service?
4. What is the basic economic problem and why does it arise?
5. Explain, with the use of a production possibility frontier, the concept of opportunity cost.
6. Choose three economic agents and explain what is meant by 'maximising behaviour'.
7. Why is economics a 'social science'? (Hint: refer to both social and science in your answer.) How do social sciences differ from other sciences you may have studied, such as chemistry or physics?
8. What is specialisation and is it always beneficial in an economic system?
9. Explain why specialisation requires a system of exchange.
10. For each of the following changes, draw a PPF showing the trade-off between output of Books and Tablets and explain the shifts or changes shown:
    (a) an improvement in technology which increases the productivity of the tablet production but leaves productivity in the book industry unchanged.
    (b) an output level which shows unemployment, or spare capacity, in the economy.
    (c) an output level where all factors of production are fully employed.
    (d) an output level which is unobtainable, or unattainable, given current factors of production.

Extension questions

A. The PPF assumes that the more specialised an economy becomes in one particular industry, the lower the productivity of each extra worker added to that industry. How does the work of Adam Smith contradict this? What does this imply for the shape of the PPF?

B. The natural environment – air, the oceans, natural habitats – often seem to be treated as a free good. Why may this not be the case?

C. Do economic agents always act rationally? Find examples of irrational behaviour and examine whether there are logical reasons behind apparently irrational behaviour.

D. Research the Global Competitiveness Report published annually by the World Economic Forum (e.g. http://www.weforum.org/reports/global-competitiveness-report-2014-2015). Which countries are the most productive? How is this related to specialisation?

E. Draw a PPF showing the trade-off between consumption goods and capital goods. Use the concept of opportunity cost to explain how lower output of consumer goods in the short-run could increase the output of both consumer goods and capital goods in the long-run.

Chapter 2
The Theory of Demand

In economics, demand is known as 'effective' demand: the amount that consumers *are willing* **and** *able* to buy of a good or service at any given price. This recognises that buyers in the market (consumers) face constraints in a world of scarce resources and cannot realistically demand infinite amounts of goods and services. A consumer's objective in an economy is therefore to maximise satisfaction (**utility**) from consumption given these constraints.

The individual demand curve

The theory of demand explains the relationship between price and quantity demanded. It is assumed that when the price of a good or service falls, the quantity demanded will increase, and vice versa. This can be seen during sales when prices are reduced and many shoppers buy more than they would have done had prices remained the same. Lower prices give consumers an incentive to increase the quantity that they demand of a good or service.

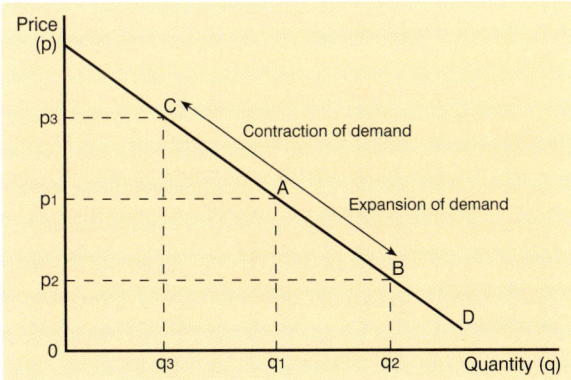

Figure 2.1: The individual demand curve

The individual demand curve (D) in Figure 2.1 shows the planned demand of a good or service at any given price for an individual consumer. It is downward sloping showing an inverse relationship between price and quantity demanded. This can be explained by the income and substitution effects. Assuming that income is fixed, a fall in the price will give the consumer an incentive to increase the quantity demanded of a good or service as the consumer has more to spend in real terms. This is called the income effect. A lower price will also make the good or service relatively cheaper than alternative goods and services (substitutes), increasing the quantity demanded. This is called the substitution effect.

The demand curve is drawn assuming that all other factors apart from price which could affect demand are held constant (ceteris paribus). In other words, price is the only variable.

A fall in price leads to an increase in quantity demanded. This is called an *expansion* of demand and is shown by a movement along the demand curve (A to B). An increase in price leads to a decrease in quantity demanded. This is called a *contraction* of demand and is shown by a movement along the demand curve (A to C).

Price is a unique determinant of demand since changes in price are shown by movements along the demand curve rather than shifting the demand curve, which occurs with non price determinants.

Diminishing marginal utility

The downward sloping demand curve can also be explained by the concept of Marginal Utility. Utility can be defined as the satisfaction from consuming a good or service and 'marginal' in Economics means additional. Imagine eating chocolate bars; the first bar offers a lot of satisfaction or utility but as more bars are eaten, each additional bar provides less utility than the previous bar. This is the theory of diminishing marginal utility which states that as more of a good or service is consumed, the utility from each additional unit (marginal utility) will decrease as shown in Figure 2.2.

Microeconomics for A Level Year 1 and AS

Figure 2.2: The marginal utility curve

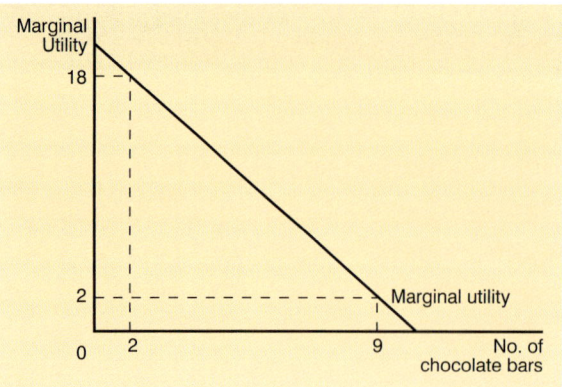

The marginal utility for two chocolate bars is 18, but by the ninth chocolate bar, it has fallen to 2. Note that the marginal utility becomes negative if too much of a good or service is consumed, leading to disutility.

This influences the shape of the demand curve, as consumers will be prepared to pay a higher price for the first unit of a good or service, which yields greater utility than consecutive units. The price that consumers are willing and able to pay is equal to the marginal utility for any given unit because they are only prepared to pay an amount that reflects the satisfaction that they get from consuming it. As the marginal utility curve is downward sloping, it can therefore be derived that the demand curve is also downward sloping.

Non-price determinants of demand

Ceteris paribus also applies to non-price determinants of demand. Each determinant is considered in isolation, assuming everything else is held constant.

Income

There is a positive relationship between income and demand. Disposable income is the amount which consumers actually have available to spend. An increase in disposable income will lead to an increase in demand at any given price and is shown by an outward shift in the demand curve.

If the government increases income tax (a direct tax paid to the government out of wages), this will decrease consumers' disposable income and lead to a decrease in demand, shown by an inward shift in the demand curve.

Wealth

There is a positive relationship between wealth and demand. Wealth can be defined as the stock of assets which has been accumulated over time. An increase in wealth increases the confidence of the consumer and leads to a positive wealth effect, whereby more is demanded and expenditure increases. An increase in wealth will lead to an increase in demand at any given price and is shown by an outward shift in the demand curve and vice versa.

Prices of other goods

Complements or complementary goods are goods or services which are purchased together, for example iPods and music from iTunes. A change in the price of one of these goods will affect the demand for another good. If the price of iPods increases (leading to a contraction of demand for iPods), this will lead to a decrease in the demand for iTunes. At every given price, less iTunes will be demanded, shown by an inward shift in the demand curve.

Substitutes are goods or services with similar uses which are in competition with each other, for example the Microsoft Xbox and the Sony PlayStation. A change in the price of one of these goods will affect the demand for another good. For example, if the price of the Microsoft Xbox increases (leading to a contraction of demand for the Xbox), this will lead to an increase in the demand for Sony PlayStations shown by an outward shift in the demand curve.

Tastes/Fashion/Advertising

Brands such as Nike may experience huge increases in demand, particularly as a result of advertising and the sponsorship of world class sports men and women which have made their products more desirable. This is shown by an outward shift in the demand curve as more of the good is demanded at every possible price. Poor image and reputation and a shift in fashions towards new goods can also damage the brand and shift demand inwards as taste for the good declines.

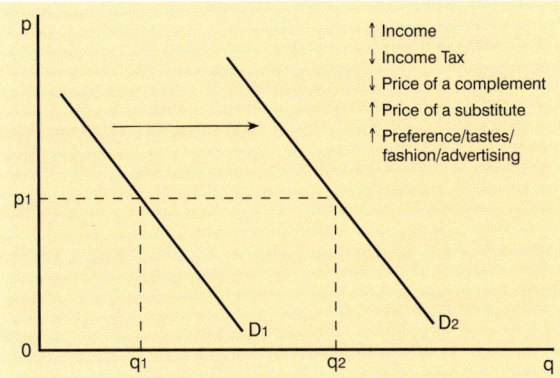

Figure 2.3: An outward shift in the demand curve

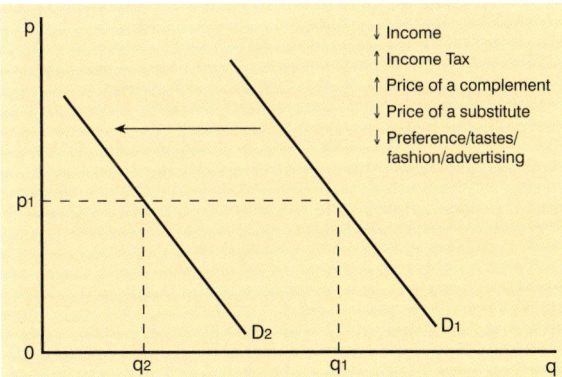

Figure 2.4: An inward shift in the demand curve

Social and emotional factors can have a strong influence on tastes and hence demand. Social media sites such as Twitter and Facebook have enabled strong trends to be set by others, influencing demand. Also an individual's state of wellbeing may affect how much is demanded, for example, if individuals are feeling confident, they may demand more and vice versa.

An outward shift illustrates an increase in demand: more of a good or service is demanded at any given price.

An inward shift illustrates a decrease in demand: less of a good or service is demanded at any given price.

Summary questions

1. What is effective demand?
2. Why is the demand curve downward sloping?
3. What is meant by an expansion or contraction of demand?
4. Explain how a change in the price of one good can affect the demand for other goods.
5. What other factors shift the demand curve?

Extension questions

A. What is the difference between an increase in demand and an increase in the quantity demanded?
B. Does the demand curve always slope downwards? Use the income and substitution effects to explain your answer.
C. Research the term Giffen good and explain how this phenomenon apppears to contradict basic principles of the laws of demand.
D. A Veblen good, or 'snob' good, is one in which a higher price signals a greater attraction to consumers. How can this be aligned with a downward-sloping demand curve?

Chapter 3
The Theory of Supply

Firms or producers in an economy supply goods and services to the market. To do this, they use factors of production and the payments incurred in the process are called costs.

It is assumed that the main objective of firms is to maximise profit. Profit is the total revenue earned from selling a good or service minus the total cost of producing it. Total revenue is calculated by price x quantity sold of a good or service.

Note that a price refers to the payment for a good or service; this is different from a cost which is a payment for a factor of production.

It is also assumed that individual firms or producers are *price takers* and have no influence on the market price, as there are many competing firms in the market. A higher price would mean no sales for a firm and a lower price would lead to insufficient profit.

The individual supply curve

The theory of supply explains the relationship between price and quantity supplied by producers in a market. It is assumed that as the price of a good or service increases, the quantity supplied increases and vice versa. Profit maximising producers will have the incentive to supply more to the market if there is a higher price, as this implies that more profit can be made by increasing production and the additional costs of doing so will be covered.

Economic theory predicts that marginal cost (the cost of producing an additional unit) will increase as more is produced. This is explained by the law of diminishing returns. Think of a room with just five computers. As more and more students come into the room and work on the computers, eventually there will be several students sharing computers and each additional student coming in will get even less work done in the short-run. (In the long-run more computers may be added to the room.) The law of diminishing returns simply states that if more of a variable factor of production such as labour is added to a fixed amount of capital, then the output (quantity) will fall for each additional worker in the short-run. Therefore, higher levels of output means increased marginal cost i.e. as output increases, the last unit becomes more and more costly to the firm due to its relative inefficiency. For each unit a higher price is therefore required to cover the increase in marginal cost and also give the producer an incentive to supply more to the market in order to maximise profit.

The individual supply curve (S) in Figure 3.1 shows the planned supply of a good or service at any given price by an individual producer. It is upward sloping due to the positive relationship between price and quantity supplied. The supply curve is drawn assuming that all other factors which could affect supply are held constant (ceteris paribus). In other words, price is the only variable.

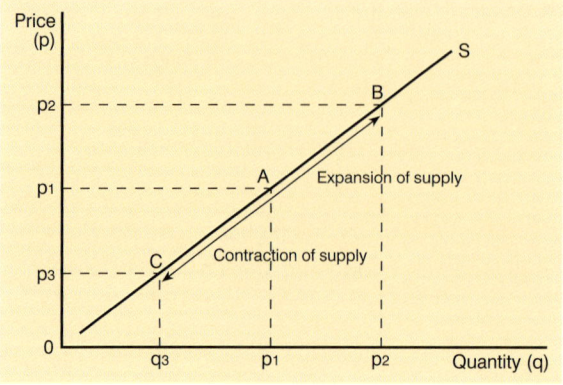

Figure 3.1: The individual supply curve

A rise in price leads to an increase in quantity supplied. This is called an *expansion* of supply and is shown by a movement along the supply curve (A to B). A decrease in price leads to a decrease in quantity supplied which is called a *contraction* of supply and is shown by a movement along the supply curve (A to C).

If the price of a commodity such as copper goes up, costs of production rise and supply decreases.

As with demand, changes in price are shown by movements along the supply curve rather than shifting the supply curve which is caused by non-price determinants.

Non-price determinants of supply

Ceteris paribus also applies to non price determinants of supply. Each determinant is considered in isolation, assuming everything else is held constant.

Costs of production

An increase in costs of production (for example as a result of an increase in the price of commodities such as copper, or higher wages paid to workers) will lead to a decrease in supply at every given price and is shown by an inward shift in the supply curve.

New technology

The development of new technology such as the internet and e-mail increases efficiency and lowers costs of production. This increases supply and is shown by an outward shift in the supply curve.

Figure 3.2: Specific tax

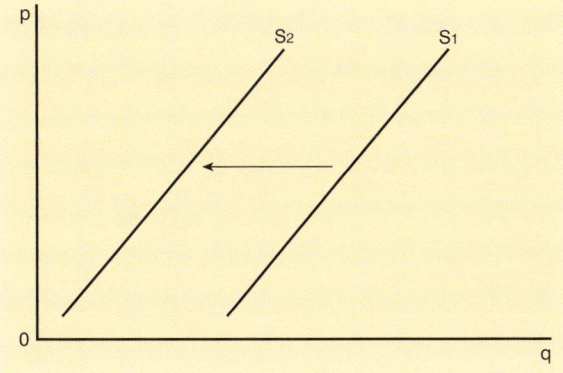

Indirect taxation

Indirect taxation is when the government places taxes on goods or services which increase a firm's costs of production and therefore decreases supply to the market. There are two types of indirect tax: specific and ad valorem.

A specific tax such as tax on cigarettes is a fixed amount per unit (box of cigarettes) and is shown by a parallel inward shift in the supply curve as shown in Figure 3.2.

Figure 3.3: Ad valorem tax

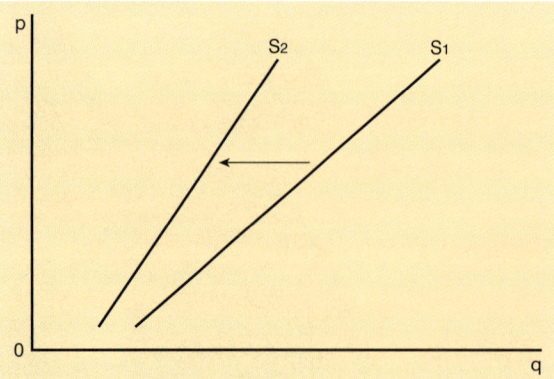

An ad valorem tax is charged as a percentage of the price of a good or service, for example Value Added Tax (VAT) is charged at 17.5% in the UK on most goods and services (with a few exceptions such as children's clothing, food, books, newspapers and magazines). An ad valorem tax is also illustrated by an inward shift but with diverging supply curves as shown in Figure 3.3.

Whilst some of these taxes are passed on to the consumer in terms of higher prices, hence the name 'indirect' tax, it is the producer who ultimately has to pay the tax to the government. It is therefore the supply curve that shifts inwards and not the demand curve.

Figure 3.4: An outward shift in the supply curve

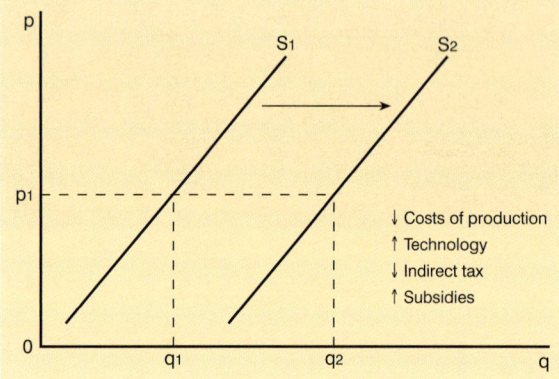

Subsidies

Subsidies are sums of money which are given by the government to producers to encourage them to supply more to the market. For example, subsidies are given to wind farms to encourage the production of greener energy. This is illustrated by an outward shift in the supply curve as in Figure 3.4.

Figure 3.5: An inward shift in the supply curve

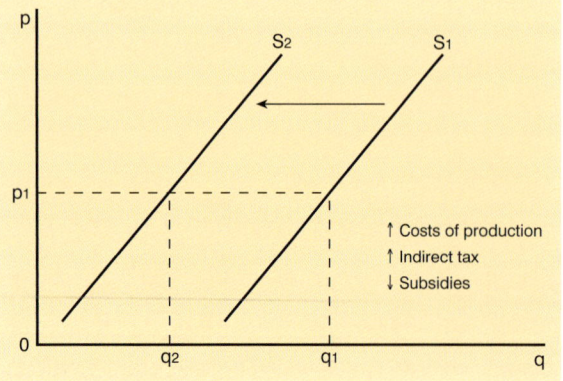

Producer cartels

Some producers will group together to control the price or quantity of a good or service. This is called a cartel. Cartels are illegal in the UK, but one global example is called the Organisation of the Petroleum Exporting Countries which consists of some of the biggest oil producing countries such as Iran, Iraq and Saudi Arabia. If the cartel decides to increase the price, then member countries will agree to restrict supply which will shift the supply curve inwards. If a decrease in price is required, then they will agree to increase supply which will shift the supply curve outwards. This is only possible if there are enough oil reserves to increase production when necessary.

An outward shift illustrates an increase in supply: more of a good or service is supplied at any given price.

An inward shift illustrates a decrease in supply: less of a good or service is supplied at any given price.

Summary questions

1. How is profit calculated?

2. Why is the supply curve upward sloping?

3. Which determinant of supply does not shift the supply curve?

4. What is the difference between a specific and an Ad Valorem tax?

5. Using diagrams and an example, explain one factor which would cause an increase in supply and one factor which would cause a decrease in supply.

Extension questions

A. Economic theory assumes that a firm's objective is to maximise profit, but are there other objectives that a firm or those who have an interest in the firm (stakeholders) might have instead?

B. To what extent does the assumption ceteris paribus make the theory of demand and supply unrealistic?

C. Analyse the effect of increasing demand from China for commodities such as oil, copper, nickel and steel on producers in the UK.

Chapter 4
Markets and Equilibrium

A market is formed when economic agents (buyers or consumers, and sellers or producers) meet to exchange goods or services. Markets can be split into three general categories; product markets (markets for goods and services), financial markets (money markets) and factor markets (markets for factors of production, such as labour). There are many sizes of markets (local markets, national markets and global markets) and different types of markets, ranging from traditional market stalls and shops to virtual markets such as eBay or Betfair. The internet has made it easier for buyers and sellers to communicate and as a result markets have become increasingly global. Many economies in the world today, including the UK, are market economies which rely on millions of markets to allocate scarce resources to produce the goods and services needed to meet peoples' wants.

Market demand and market supply curves

Demand and supply curves can be applied to both individuals and markets. A market demand curve is simply all the individual consumers' demand curves for a good or service added together. This is shown very simply in Figure 4.1 which assumes the market has two individuals, A and B. Whilst individual demand curves are not identical, they are assumed to be predominantly downward sloping, therefore in economic theory, the market demand curve is downward sloping.

Figure 4.1: Individual and market demand curves

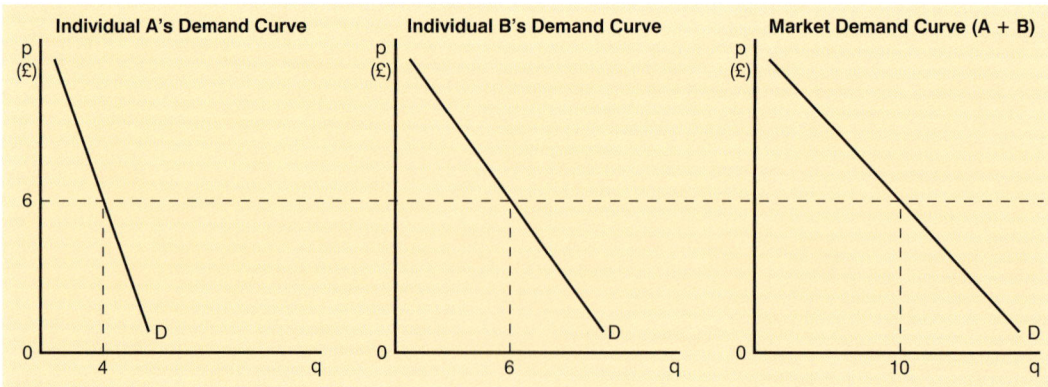

Similarly a market supply curve is all the individual producers' supply curves for a good or service added together. The table below shows simply the total supply for a market with two producers.

Price (£)	Producer A (units)	Producer B (units)	Total Supply (units)
1	6	4	10
2	8	6	14
3	10	8	18
4	12	10	22

It is assumed that individual supply curves are predominantly upward sloping and therefore the market supply curve is also upward sloping.

Market equilibrium

Market equilibrium is achieved when planned demand is equal to planned supply and there is no incentive for buyers or sellers to change their market plans. There is no excess demand or excess supply. Excess demand (shortage) occurs when quantity demanded is greater than quantity supplied. Excess supply (glut) occurs when quantity supplied is greater than quantity demanded. If excess demand or supply exists then the market is in disequilibrium.

Figure 4.2: Market equilibrium

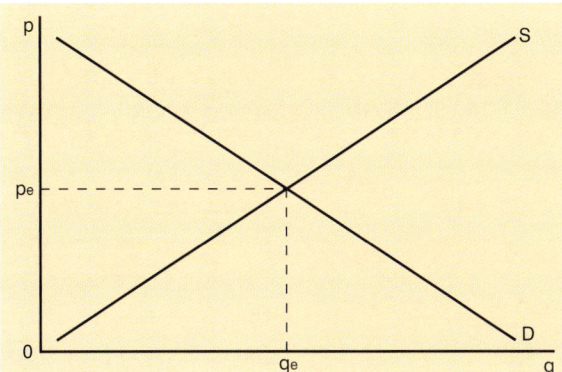

Figure 4.2 shows a market in equilibrium. The price and quantity may be referred to as the equilibrium or market clearing price (p_e) and quantity (q_e).

The functions of price and the allocation of scarce resources

Markets have an important role in solving the economic problem. Scarce resources can be allocated efficiently via the price mechanism (the interaction between supply and demand which determines the price and therefore quantity of a good or service in a market). It is assumed that markets are competitive in which consumers and producers have perfect information and follow their own self interests. The price mechanism consists of three functions of price which ensure that a free market (a market with no government intervention) will always end up in equilibrium.

1. **Signalling function** – prices carry information which is used by consumers and producers to make their market plans.

2. **Rationing or Allocative function** – this function reflects the economic problem. If there is scarcity in the market i.e. excess demand, then the price will increase as consumers bid up the price in order to be able to obtain the good or service. This will reduce the quantity demanded in the market and therefore scarce goods are rationed or allocated via a higher price.

3. **Incentive function** – producers have the objective of maximising profit. Profit therefore has an important role in terms of allocating resources as it is assumed to be the driving force of producers and determines their market plans. The higher the price, the greater the opportunity there is to increase profit and therefore producers have an incentive to increase the quantity supplied to the market. Consumers on the other hand, have the objective of maximising utility (satisfaction), therefore a lower price will give them an incentive to increase the quantity demanded.

Figure 4.3: The elimination of excess demand

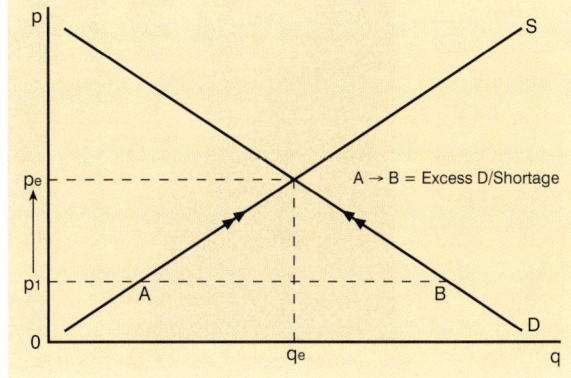

To see the price mechanism in action, there are two different circumstances in the market to consider: excess demand (shortage) and excess supply (glut), both of which occur when there is disequilibrium i.e. when planned demand is not equal to planned supply.

Excess demand is eliminated via the following market clearing process. At the current price p_1 in Figure 4.3, the quantity demanded is greater than the quantity supplied. However,

this situation is not sustainable as consumers will follow their self interest which is to maximise utility. Consumers bid up the price against each other in order to obtain the good or service. This has a *rationing* effect as some consumers who can no longer afford the higher price leave the market. The overall effect is that the quantity demanded falls as the price increases (a contraction of demand). Increases in price *signal* information to producers that there has been a change in the market. Producers will also follow their self interest, which is to maximise profit. A higher price therefore gives producers an *incentive* to increase the quantity supplied (an expansion of supply). The process continues until the quantity demanded is equal to quantity supplied and equilibrium is reached, with a higher equilibrium price (p_e) and corresponding quantity (q_e).

Figure 4.4: The elimination of excess supply

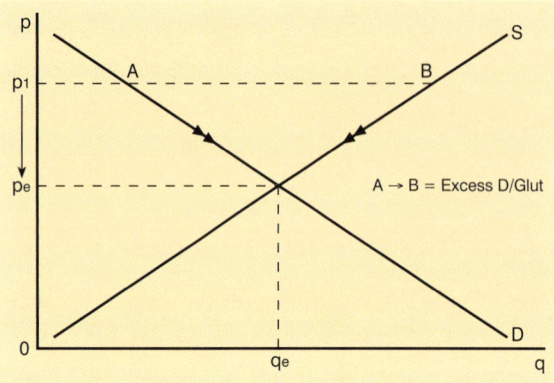

Excess supply can also be eliminated via the price mechanism. At the current price p1 in Figure 4.4, the quantity supplied is greater than the quantity demanded. Therefore producers who have stocks of unsold goods will reduce their prices in order to try and sell them. Some producers will make a loss and leave the market because they no longer have an *incentive* to produce, reducing the quantity supplied to the market (a contraction of supply). Then the *signalling* function of price leads to consumers changing their plans based on the information they receive from falling prices. The falling price reflects a reduction in *scarcity* (the rationing function) and gives consumers an *incentive* to increase the quantity demanded. The process continues until the quantity demanded is equal to quantity supplied and equilibrium is reached, with a lower equilibrium price of p_e and corresponding quantity q_e.

Adam Smith described the movement to equilibrium as the '**Invisible Hand**' of market forces. Whilst this is a strange term, it reflects the fact that markets require no government intervention to reach equilibrium. Free market economies can therefore in theory achieve an efficient allocation of resources. Economic actors simply need to compete against each other and follow their self interest: Perfect competition is an important assumption in order for the free market to allocate resources efficiently. A perfectly competitive market is one in which there are many firms in the market all producing the same good or service and each individual firm is not large enough to influence the market price: they must accept the equilibrium price determined by the price mechanism (also referred to as the market mechanism). There is also perfect information.

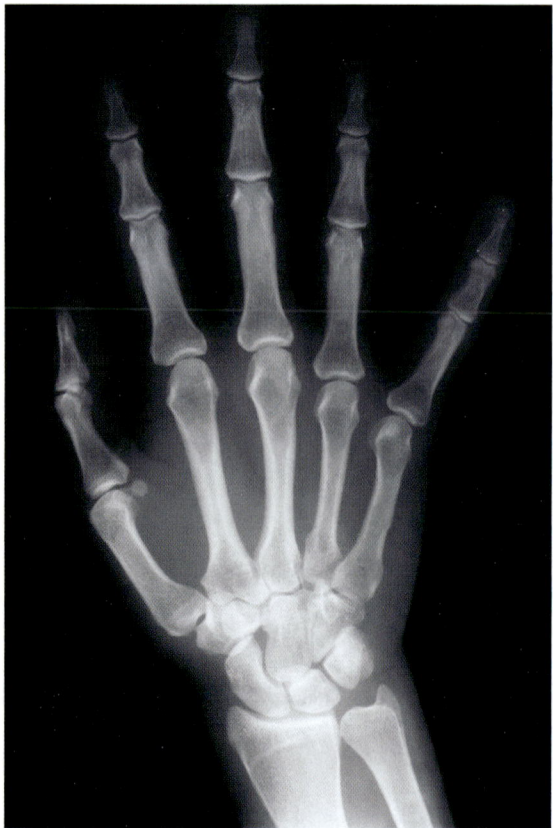

Adam Smith described the movement to equilibrium as the 'invisible hand' of market forces.

Causes of disequilibrium

Disequilibrium, caused by excess demand or supply, can occur temporarily in markets as a result of a change in demand or supply, whilst economic agents adjust their plans according to the signalling function of price. It can also be as a result of a deliberate intervention by the government, for example maximum prices which artificially hold the price below the equilibrium (leading to excess demand) and minimum prices which artificially hold the price above the equilibrium (leading to excess supply). Trade unions can use collective bargaining power to increase the wage in the labour market, leading to disequilibrium as discussed in Chapter 6.

Changes in equilibrium

Changes in non-price determinants of demand and/or supply will lead to a market moving to a new equilibrium.

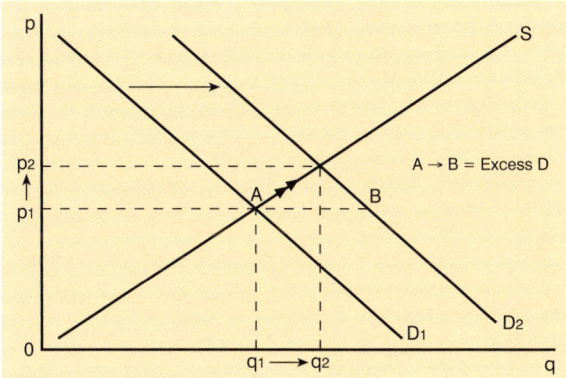

Figure 4.5: The effect on the market of an increase in demand

An increase in the demand for petrol caused by a decrease in price of cars will shift the demand curve outwards from D1 to D2 as shown by Figure 4.5. This is because petrol and cars are complementary goods. At p1 the increase in demand leads to excess demand which is eliminated by the price mechanism. The equilibrium price increases from p1 to p2 and the equilibrium quantity increases from q1 to q2. Note that an increase in demand leads to an expansion of supply.

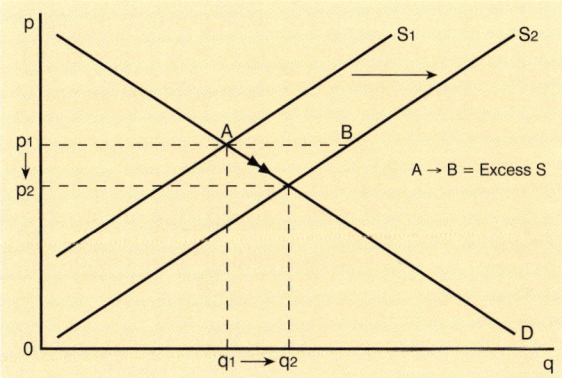

Figure 4.6: The effect on the market of an increase in supply

An increase in the supply of flat screen TVs due to the development of new technology will shift the supply curve outwards from S1 to S2 as shown in Figure 4.6. At p1 the increase in supply leads to excess supply which is eliminated by the price mechanism. The equilibrium price falls from p1 to p2 and the equilibrium quantity increases from q1 to q2. An increase in supply leads to an expansion of demand.

Consumer surplus

Consumer surplus is the difference between how much consumers in the market are prepared to pay (as shown by the demand curve) and how much they actually pay (the equilibrium price).

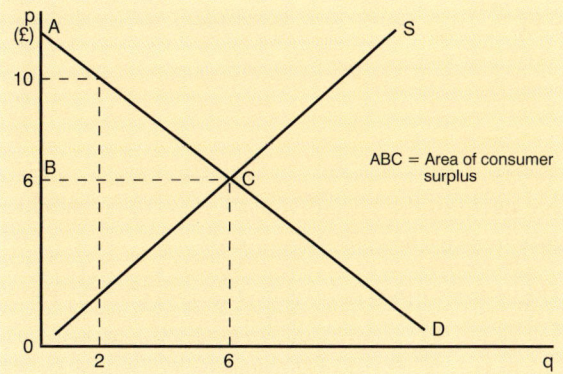

Figure 4.7: Consumer surplus

The consumer surplus per unit is the vertical difference between the price given by the demand curve for that quantity and the equilibrium price. Figure 4.7 shows that at a quantity of 2 units, the consumer is willing to pay £10 but only actually pays £6, therefore there is a gain of £4. At equilibrium consumer

Figure 4.8: Change in consumer surplus caused by an increase in supply

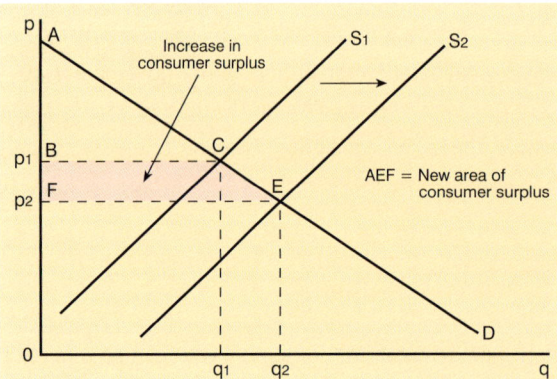

Figure 4.9: Calculating consumer surplus

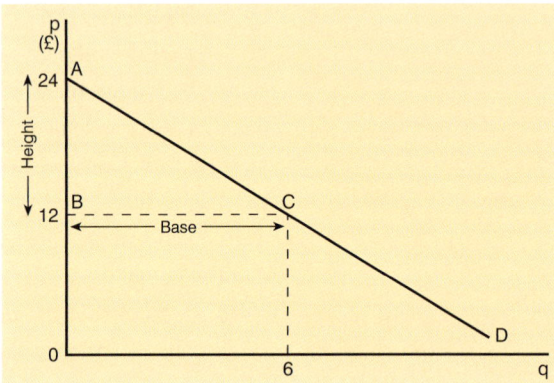

Figure 4.10: Calculating change in consumer surplus due to a fall in price

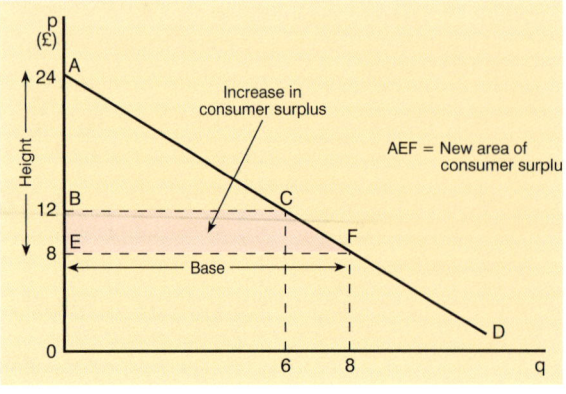

surplus is maximised as the amount a consumer is willing to pay is equal to the amount they actually pay (in this case £6 at a quantity of 6 units). The area of consumer surplus is therefore given by ABC.

Changes in consumer surplus

A change in consumer surplus will occur if there is a change in equilibrium price. For example, if there is an increase in supply, as shown in Figure 4.8, the consumer surplus will increase by the shaded area BCEF. The new area of consumer surplus is now AEF.

Calculating consumer surplus and changes in consumer surplus

Consumer surplus can be calculated by finding the area of the triangle ABC as shown in Figure 4.9. The area of a triangle is calculated by the formula ½ (base x height). Therefore if the price is £12 and quantity demanded is 6 units, the consumer surplus can be calculated in the following way. The base is simply given by the quantity, 6 units. The height is the difference between the point at which the demand curve cuts the y axis and the price, i.e. 24 - 12 = 12. Therefore the area of the triangle is ½ (6 x 12) = £36

If the price falls to £8 and the quantity demanded increases to 8 units, as shown in Figure 4.10, the same method can be used to find the new area of consumer surplus AEF

Base = 8

Height = 24 - 8 = 16

Consumer surplus = ½ (16 x 8) = £64

Change of consumer surplus = 64 - 36 = £28

Consumer surplus has increased by £28 as a result of a decrease in price. This increase is shown by the shaded area in Figure 4.10.

Producer surplus

Producer surplus is the difference between the price that producers are prepared to sell their good or service and how much they actually receive (the equilibrium price).

The producer surplus per unit is the vertical difference between the price given by the supply curve for that quantity and the equilibrium price. Figure 4.11 shows that at a quantity of 2 units, the producer is willing to sell their goods for a price of £2 but actually receives the equilibrium price of £8, therefore gaining £6.

Figure 4.11: Producer surplus

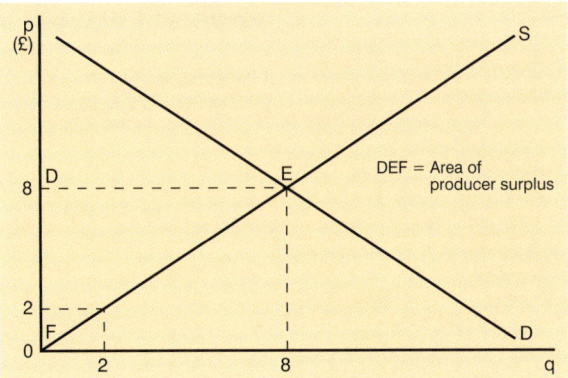

At equilibrium, producer surplus is maximised as the price a producer is willing to sell for is equal to the amount they actually receive (in this case £8 at a quantity of 8 units). The area of producer surplus is therefore given by DEF.

Figure 4.12: Change in producer surplus caused by an increase in demand

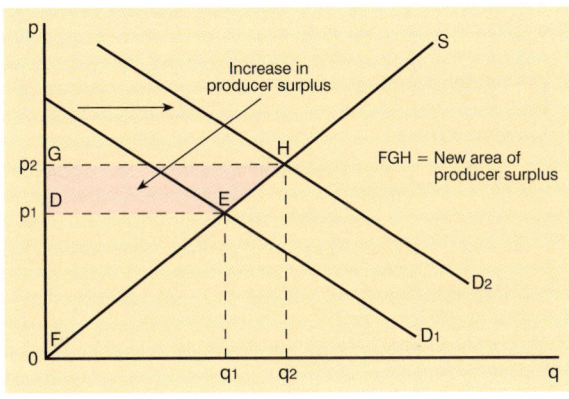

Changes in producer surplus

A change in producer surplus will occur if there is a change in equilibrium price. For example, if there is an increase in demand, as shown in Figure 4.12, the producer surplus will increase by the shaded area DEHG. The new area of consumer surplus is now GHF.

Figure 4.13: Calculating producer surplus and change in producer surplus due to an increase in price

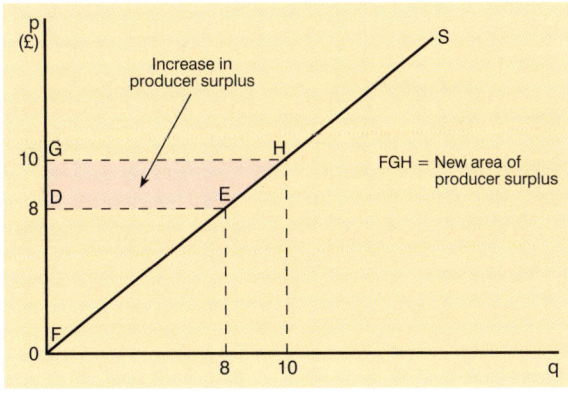

Calculating producer surplus and changes in producer surplus

Producer surplus can be calculated by finding the area of the triangle DEF as shown in Figure 4.13, in which there is a price of £8 and a quantity of 8 units. The producer surplus is therefore simply ½ (8 x 8) = £32.

If the price increases to £10 and the quantity supplied increases to 10 units, the same method can be used to find the new area of producer surplus FGH i.e. ½ (10 x 10) = £50.

An increase in price leads to an increase in producer surplus, in this case by £18. This increase is shown by the shaded area in Figure 4.13.

A change in price will therefore always create winners and losers, in terms of consumers and producers. If the price falls, consumers benefit and if the price increases, producers benefit.

Microeconomics for A Level Year 1 and AS

Figure 4.14: Consumer surplus and producer surplus at equilibrium

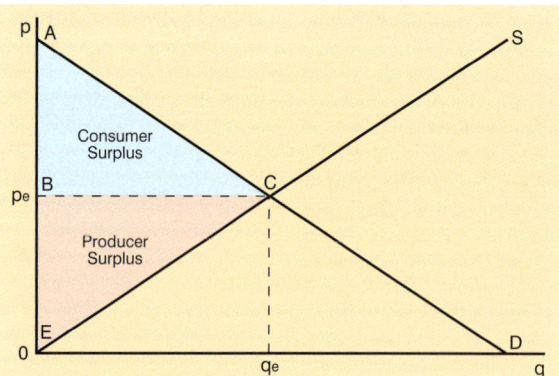

Consumer surplus and producer surplus at equilibrium

Figure 4.14 shows consumer and producer surplus are both maximised at equilibrium.

Summary questions

1. What is meant by a free market?
2. How does a free market economy allocate scarce resources?
3. Explain the term market equilibrium.
4. Using a diagram, show how a fall in the price of Apple Macs affects the equilibrium in the market for PCs.
5. Using Figure 4.15, clearly show the consumer and producer surplus at equilibrium price p1. Show the impact of an increase in price on both consumer and producer surplus.

Starting each time from a copy of Figure 4.15, show the impact of each of the following on equilibrium and quantity.

6. a rise in the price of a substitute.
7. a fall in the costs of production.
8. an increase in the rate of an indirect tax such as VAT.
9. a shift in taste away from a good towards a rival product.
10. Using a diagram showing the market for bus journeys, explain how a rise in the price of car insurance *and* a fall in bus drivers' wages can have *two* possible impacts on the price of bus journeys.

Figure 4.15

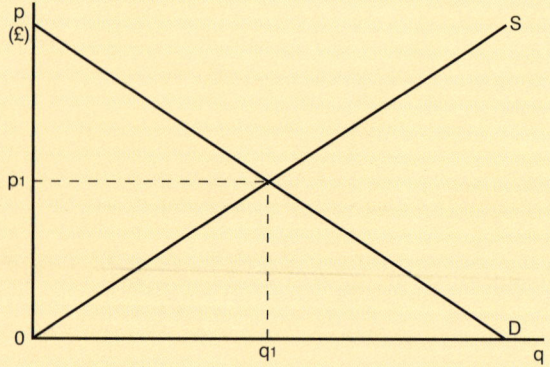

Extension questions

A. Why might agricultural markets exhibit price volatility?

B. Research the market for oil and the role of OPEC. Does OPEC increase or decrease the stability of prices in the oil market?

C. Research the ideas of Adam Smith, who is often claimed as an economist whose work supports unregulated, free markets. To what extent does Smith deserve this reputation?

Chapter 5
Elasticity

Previous chapters have shown how changes in price result in movements along the demand and supply curves, and how changes in non-price factors can shift the position of one curve or the other.

Elasticity is a means of quantifying these changes: putting values to the increases and decreases in demand, supply, quantity demanded and quantity supplied.

Elasticity: definitions

Elasticity measures the responsiveness of one variable to a change in another variable. We will examine four key elasticities in this chapter:

Price Elasticity of Demand (PED) measures the responsiveness of quantity demanded to a change in price

Cross Price Elasticity of Demand (XED) measures the responsiveness of demand to a change in the price of another good

Income Elasticity of Demand (YED) measures the responsiveness of demand to a change in income

Price Elasticity of Supply (PES) measures the responsiveness of quantity supplied to a change in price

Price Elasticity of Demand (PED)

The demand curve shows the relationship between price and quantity demanded. Price Elasticity of Demand (PED) quantifies this relationship and is calculated by the formula:

$$\text{Price Elasticity of Demand} = \frac{\% \text{ change in quantity demanded}}{\% \text{ change in price}} = \frac{\%\Delta Q_d}{\%\Delta P}$$

Demand curves with different PED are shown in Figures 5.1 and 5.2.

In both cases, price increases from p_1 to p_2. In Figure 5.1 a large increase in price leads to a small fall in quantity demanded; in Figure 5.2 a small increase in price causes a large fall in quantity demanded. Thus demand in Figure 5.1 is price inelastic, or relatively unresponsive to changes in price, and in Figure 5.2 is price elastic, or more responsive to changes in price.

The formula for PED allows this responsiveness to be quantified. For example, if a 10% increase in price causes only a 5% fall in quantity demanded, PED is (5%/10%) which equals 0.5.

Figure 5.1: Price inelastic demand

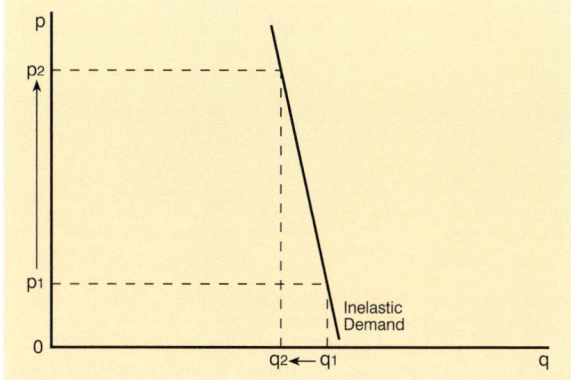

In fact, PED should really be expressed as a negative number as a fall in price (-) causes an increase in quantity (+) and vice versa, but economists generally write it without the minus sign (please note that this is not true for the other elasticities, where the sign is important!)

Inelastic demand occurs where PED < 1.

Elastic demand occurs where PED > 1.

Unit elasticity occurs where PED = 1.

Figure 5.2: Price elastic demand

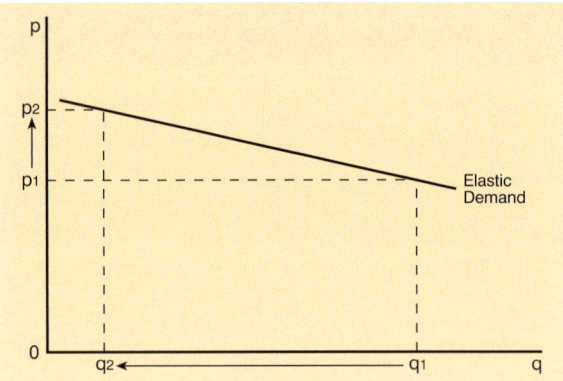

Calculating PED using point elasticity

Figure 5.3: PED along a straight line demand schedule

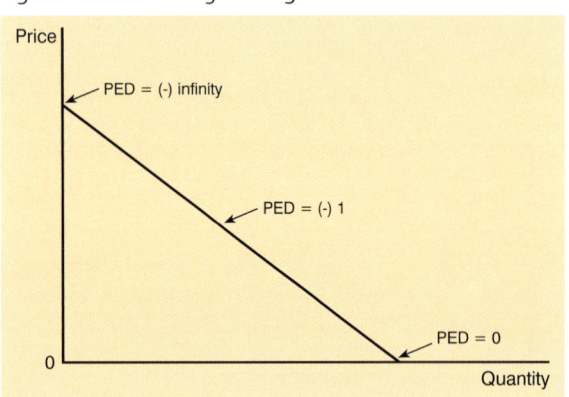

Technically, the price elasticity of demand differs along a straight line demand curve, from infinity where the line cuts the price axis to zero where the line cuts the quantity axis. At exactly half way along the demand schedule, PED will be (-) 1.

The use of point elasticity can be used to resolve examples where numerical examples produce different results when a price increases compared to when a price falls, as in the following example:

Price	£10	£15
Quantity	1000	500

In this case, when the price is increased from £10 to £15, PED is (% change in Q / % change in P) = (-50% / 50%) = (-) 1

However, if the price is reduced from £15 to £10, PED is (+ 100% / -33.3%) = (-) 3

Point elasticity uses average levels and changes, as follows:

Point Elasticity = $\dfrac{\text{average P}}{\text{average Q}} \times \dfrac{\text{change in Q}}{\text{change in P}}$

which for this example is:

$$\dfrac{£12.50}{750} \times \dfrac{-500}{+£5}$$

$$= \dfrac{-£6250}{3750}$$

$$= \mathbf{-1.67} \text{ (2 decimal places)}$$

The point halfway along a straight line demand schedule, where point elasticity of demand equals (-) 1 is also the price and quantity combination where total revenue (P x Q) is maximised.

Determinants of PED

The price elasticity of demand for a good is determined by four factors:

1. The degree of necessity of the good
2. The number of substitutes available
3. The time available to find effective substitutes
4. The proportion of income spent on the good

Degree of necessity

When fuel bills increase, households have little choice but to keep paying for the service (although some attempt to economise on gas and electricity use may be made). If the price of foreign holidays increased dramatically, on the other hand, many households would seek cheaper domestic alternatives. Thus demand would be price inelastic in the first instance and price elastic in the second.

Availability of substitutes

The more substitutes there are available, the higher PED will be and thus the more price elastic demand becomes. This can be illustrated by considering the market for food (which is very price inelastic) compared to the market for bread (which is more elastic, as substitutes such as rice and pasta exist) and then the market for a brand of bread (which is even more elastic, as many substitutes exist in the form of other brands of bread).

Time

If you arrive at the train station to see that fares have risen overnight you have little choice but to pay the higher price (assuming you are sufficiently motivated to get to your destination). But over time you are able to consider alternatives (buying a bike or a car, moving to within walking distance of school/work/the pub) and thus demand tends to become more price elastic over time, providing realistic substitutes can be found.

Proportion of income spent on the good

An increase in the price of chewing gum is unlikely to affect a household's budget significantly, but an increase in the price of petrol or domestic heating bills might. Thus where the price rise is less significant, the expected reaction will be far less than where the higher price has a far greater impact on overall spending.

PED and Total Revenue

Total Revenue is calculated as price multiplied by quantity demanded. This shows two things: the money (or revenue) received by the supplier, and total spending (or total expenditure) by consumers on this good.

If a firm changes the price of their good this may increase revenue, decrease revenue or keep revenue constant. The determinant of which of these occurs is PED.

For example, if a firm raises the price of a good by 5%, this means that for every unit sold, they gain 5% higher revenue. However, the increase in price will reduce the willingness and ability of consumers to purchase the good. If quantity demanded falls by 10%, for example, the price rise (which increases revenue) is combined with a 10% fall in sales (which reduces revenue). This may be best illustrated using a numerical example:

Let us assume that the old price is £100, at which 400 units are bought. If price rises by 5% the new price is £105, but quantity demanded falls by 10% to 360 units. This total revenue falls from (£100 x 400 = £40,000) to (£105 x 360 = £37,800).

Conversely, if the percentage increase in price is higher than the percentage fall in quantity demanded, total revenue will rise.

Figure 5.4: Price fall, price inelastic demand

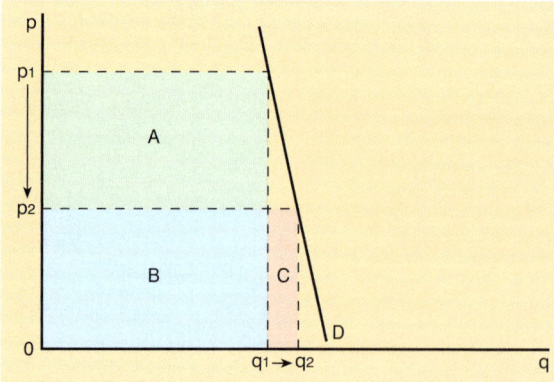

Figure 5.5: Price fall, price elastic demand

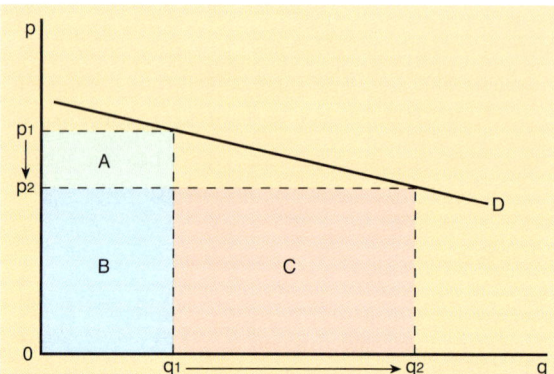

Figures 5.4 and 5.5 show this for decreases in price from p1 to p2 in each case. Total revenue is shown as the shaded area with a height of price and a length of quantity demanded in each case.

In Figure 5.4 the total revenue at price p1 is shown by the area A + B, and at price p2 by the area B + C. Area B is in common at both prices, but the result of the price cut is that the loss of revenue (area A) is greater than the increase in revenue (area C) resulting from slightly higher sales. Thus total revenue falls by the difference between area A and area C.

In Figure 5.5 the total revenue levels are also shown, but this time the loss of revenue resulting from the lower price (area A) is outweighed by the increase in revenue resulting from proportionately higher sales (area C). Thus total revenue rises by the difference between area A and area C.

The relationship between price changes, total revenue and price elasticity of demand is shown in Table 5.1.

Table 5.1: The relationship between price changes, PED and total revenue

	↑ Price	↓ Price
PED > 1 Price Elastic Demand	Total Revenue ↓	Total Revenue ↑
PED = 1 Unitary Price Elastic Demand	Total Revenue unchanged	Total Revenue unchanged
PED < 1 Price Inelastic Demand	Total Revenue ↑	Total Revenue ↓

PED and Indirect Taxation

PED is also important when considering the impact of indirect taxes on production and consumption levels. The government often taxes goods which are deemed undesirable (see later chapters on demerit goods and negative externalities) but the effectiveness of these taxes in reducing quantity demanded will be determined to some extent by the PED.

Figure 5.6: Indirect tax and price elastic demand

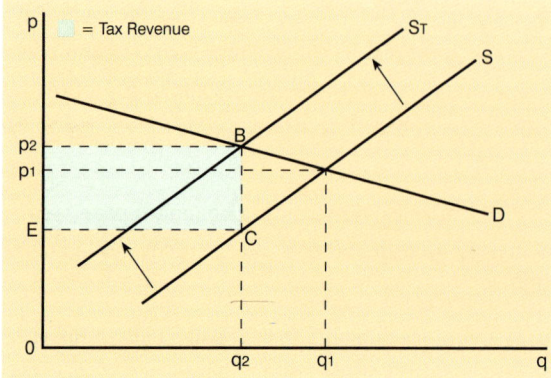

The more price inelastic demand is, the less effective an indirect tax will be in reducing use of the good. This is particularly true of goods with few or no substitutes, where use of the good is habitual or habit-forming (e.g. private car use, addictive drugs), and where

Figure 5.7: Indirect tax and price inelastic demand

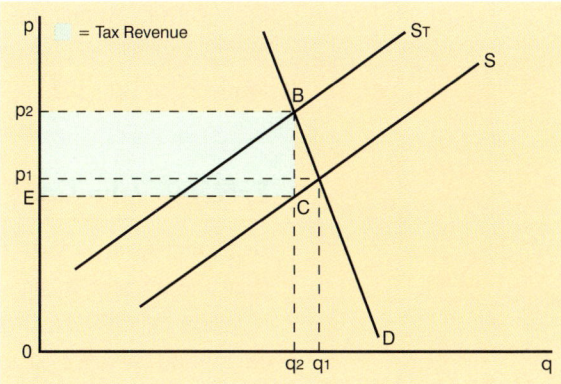

the good forms a relatively small proportion of overall spending.

However, indirect taxes are very effective at raising revenue when demand is price inelastic. Figures 5.6 and 5.7 compare the impact of an indirect tax on goods with different price inelasticities.

Although quantity falls from q_1 to q_2 in both cases as the supply curve shifts back from S to S_T, this fall is much smaller when demand is price inelastic. The tax revenue generated (the area bounded by the points p2BCE on both diagrams) is, however, greater when demand is price inelastic. This is because the firm is able to pass on far more of the tax to the consumer without seeing a large drop in sales.

Figure 5.8: Subsidy and price elastic demand

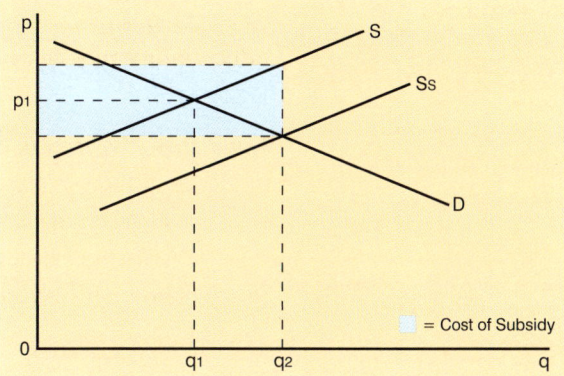

Similarly, subsidies from the government to increase provision of a good will shift the supply curve outwards from S to S_S and will be most effective where demand is price elastic – but the cost of the subsidy will be greater, as can be seen when comparing Figures 5.8 and 5.9.

Figure 5.9: Subsidy and price inelastic demand

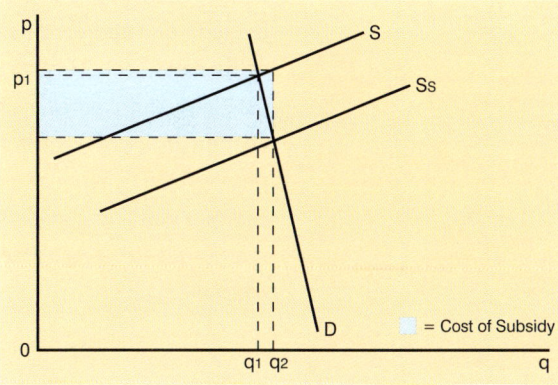

An important consideration when using taxes and subsidies to change prices and output levels is the incidence of the tax. Incidence refers to who pays the tax. In most cases, an indirect tax is paid in part by both the producer and consumer, as shown on Figure 5.10.

The imposition of an indirect tax shifts the supply curve inwards from S to S_T. The tax per unit (shown by the vertical distance between the two supply curves) is paid by the producers to the government, thereby increasing the cost of production. Producers however can pass on some of the tax on to the consumer in terms of a higher price. The tax increases the price for each unit supplied from p_1 to p_2 and this is referred to as the consumer incidence of the tax: the increase in price experienced by consumers. The remainder of the tax per unit is called the producer incidence of the tax, shown by the vertical distance $p_1 - p_3$.

Figure 5.10: Consumer and producer incidence of indirect taxation

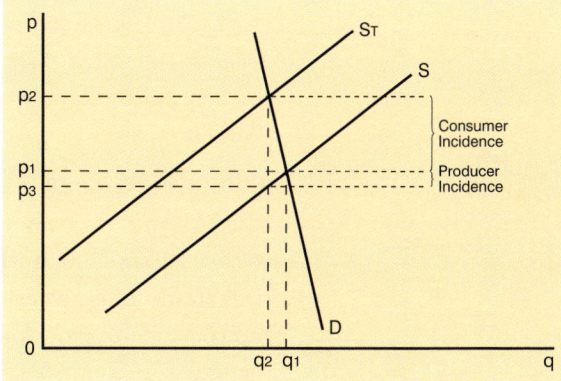

The more price elastic the demand for the good, the less of the tax the producer can

Figure 5.11: Consumer and producer incidence and price inelastic demand

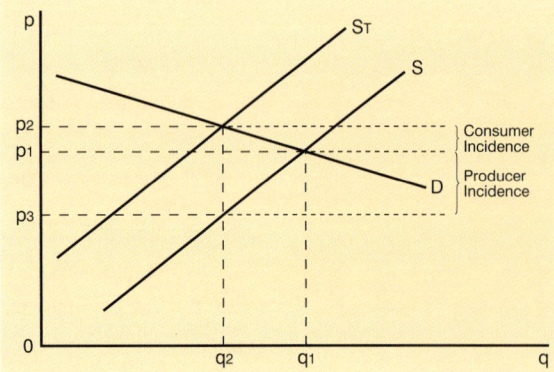

pass on to consumers. This is shown in Figure 5.11, with consumer incidence of (p2 - p1) being much lower than the producer incidence of (p1 - p3).

Extreme values of PED

Demand may be perfectly price elastic, where even the smallest change in price will either reduce demand to zero (if price rises) or create an infinite increase (if price falls). This is shown on Figure 5.12.

Demand may be perfectly price inelastic, where even large changes in price have no effect on quantity demanded, as shown in Figure 5.13.

Figure 5.12: Perfectly price elastic demand

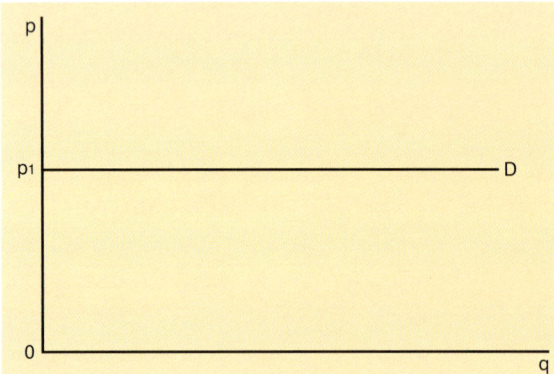

Note that the consumer and producer incidence of taxes in these two cases above will fall entirely on the producer (when there is perfectly elastic demand) and the consumer (when there is perfectly inelastic demand).

The importance of price elasticity of demand for the implications of a price change in total revenue was explored earlier in this chapter. It is also possible for a demand curve (or at least a region of a curve) to have a price elasticity of demand of 1. This is called unitary price elasticity and creates a situation where any change in price is exactly matched by a proportionate change in quantity. Figure 5.14 shows a demand curve where, regardless of the output (q) level chosen, total revenue is constant.

Figure 5.13: Perfectly price inelastic demand

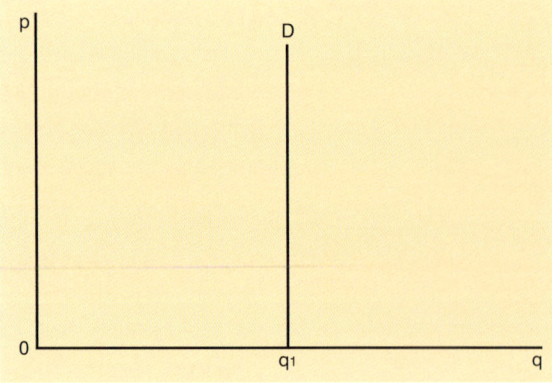

Income Elasticity of Demand (YED)

Income elasticity of demand measures the responsiveness of demand to a change in income. Income is a non-price determinant of demand, and thus a change in income shifts the demand curve outwards or inwards as shown in Figure 5.15.

A change in income will affect the demand for different types of goods in different ways. If you were given £100 to spend, you would be likely to spend this on entertainment, drinks and computer games. Similarly, a household winning a sum on the lottery will increase

Figure 5.14: Unitary price elasticity of demand

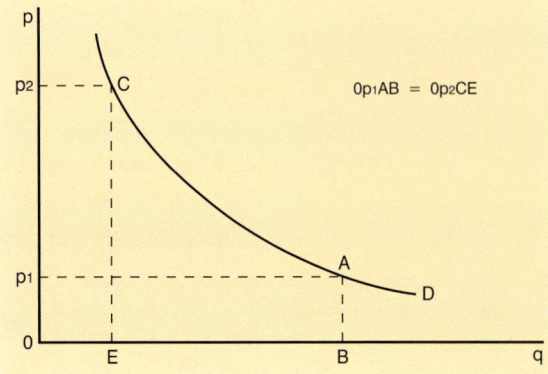

Figure 5.15: Income and demand, normal goods

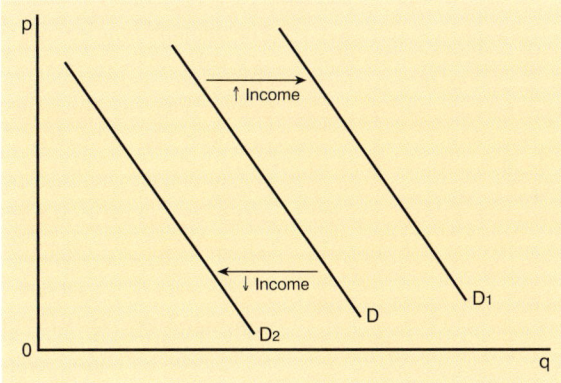

Figure 5.16: Increased income and demand for bread

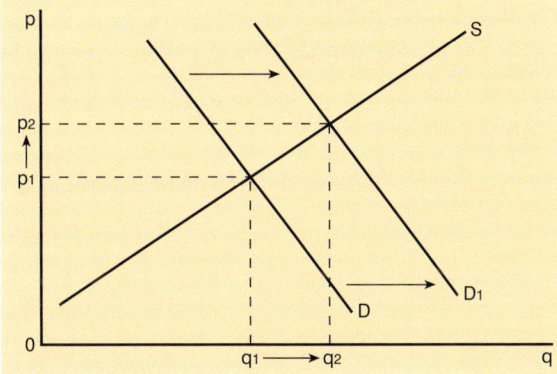

Figure 5.17: Increased income and demand for foreign holidays

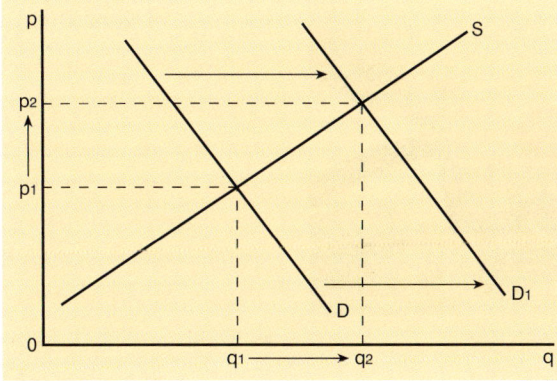

Figure 5.18: Increased income and inferior goods

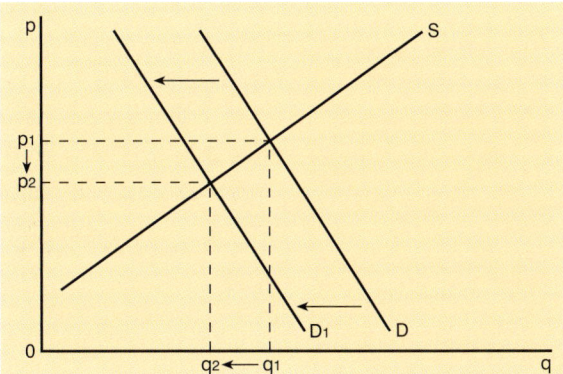

demand for foreign holidays, new cars, expensive clothes and electrical goods far more than the demand for, say, salt or bread.

Figures 5.16 and 5.17 show the impact of higher incomes on two goods: bread and holidays. Although both goods experience an increase in demand as a result of higher incomes, the increase in the demand for holidays is far greater.

Goods such as holidays are **luxuries** or **superior goods** and have an income elasticity of demand greater than 1.

Goods such as bread are **necessities** or **basic goods** and have an income elasticity of demand between 0 and 1.

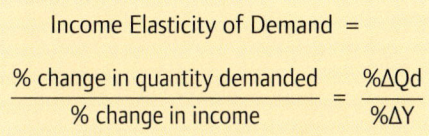

Luxuries and necessities are referred to by economists as normal goods: as income rises, demand for normal goods increases, albeit to different degrees.

Another type of good is an inferior good. When income rises, the demand for inferior goods falls, as shown in Figure 5.18.

Inferior goods are easily identifiable for an individual consumer or household. Students leaving university and getting their first job may eat fewer meals of baked beans on toast and more chicken or steak! Similarly, public transport may be consumed less as car use increases.

Examples of inferior goods across an economy are controversial. Even if incomes rise across all households equally, some people may choose to drive rather than take a bus, but for other households bus travel may increase, for example for recreation as well as travelling to work.

Microeconomics for A Level Year 1 and AS

Cross Price Elasticity of Demand (XED)

Figure 5.19: Changes in the price of complements and substitutes

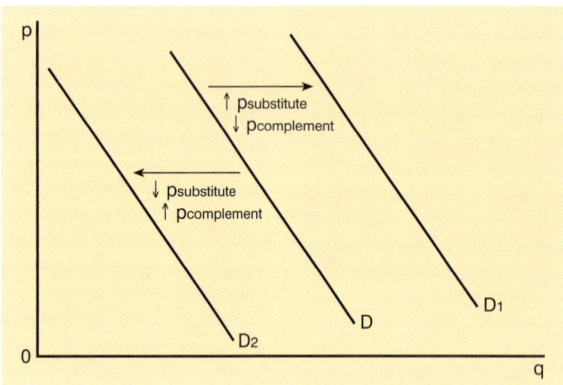

The demand for a good is determined by both the price of the good and the price of other goods. For example, the demand for DVD players will be influenced not only by the price of the players, but also by the price of DVD disks. This is a situation of **joint demand**, where two (or more) goods are demanded to be *used together*. These goods are **complements**. Other examples include cars and petrol, and hotel rooms and flights.

The demand for a DVD player will also be determined by alternatives. A consumer wishing to watch a film could also go to the cinema or watch TV instead. Alternatively, they could use their leisure time in a different way, for instance by listening to the radio or going to the pub. This is called **competitive demand** and goods which are used *instead of each other* are called **substitutes**.

Changes in the prices of complements and substitutes will shift the demand curve as shown in Figure 5.19.

The impact of these changes can be quantified with cross elasticity of demand. This is a measure of the responsiveness of demand to a change in the price of complements and substitutes. The formula is:

$$\text{Cross Price Elasticity of Demand} = \frac{\%\text{ change in quantity demanded of good A}}{\%\text{ change in price of good B}} = \frac{\%\Delta Qa}{\%\Delta Pb}$$

The increase in the price of petrol causes a fall in the demand for cars.

Figure 5.20: The meaning of values of XED

Goods which are unrelated will have a cross price elasticity (XED) of zero – the change in the price of good B has no impact on the quantity demanded of good A.

Complements have a negative cross price elasticity: the increase in the price of petrol causes a fall in the demand for cars. This magnitude of XED (the size of the number, ignoring the sign) shows the strength of the relationship, with a number between 0 and 1 showing a weak XED and a number higher than 1 (or lower than -1) showing strong XED.

Similarly, substitutes have positive XED. If the price of one brand of soft drink falls, the demand for a competing brand will fall. Again, the magnitude is important. An XED higher than 1 shows the goods are strong substitutes, a value between 0 and 1 means the goods are weak substitutes.

The values of XED are summarised in Figure 5.20.

Price Elasticity of Supply (PES)

Price elasticity of supply measures the responsiveness of quantity supplied to changes in price. PES differs from PED, YED and XED as it models the behaviour of firms rather than the behaviour of consumers. The formula is:

$$\text{Price Elasticity of Supply} = \frac{\%\text{ change in quantity supplied}}{\%\text{ change in price}} = \frac{\%\Delta Q_s}{\%\Delta P}$$

As price and quantity supplied are (generally) positively related, the value of PES is usually positive. However, it may be very low, or even zero, in some circumstances.

PES and time scale

Firms respond to incentives, and their main incentive to increase their supply of a good to the market is a higher price. For example, if your economics teacher paid you to write essays at a rate of £1 per page, you would produce the length of work which represented a satisfactory reward (number of pages x £1) versus the opportunity cost of your time (is £1 sufficient reward for the time and effort required to write another page?). Ceteris paribus, an increase in the reward for your work (e.g. a pay rise to £2 per page) would lead to higher quantity supplied. Hence the upward-sloping supply curve and positive price elasticity of supply (see Figure 5.21).

Figure 5.21: Price elasticity of supply in action

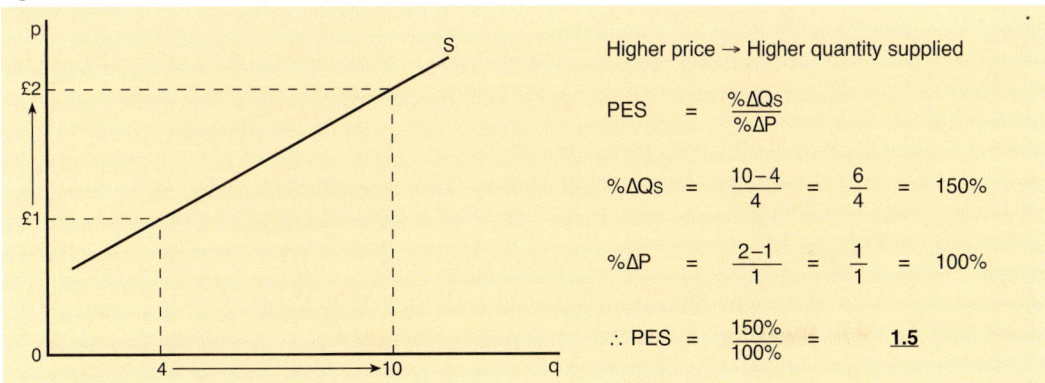

However, what if you only heard about the increase in reward as you entered the lesson in which your essay was due to be handed in? With no time to supply more pages, your supply curve would be vertical, even if the price rose to £3 or £30. This is true at any point where a supplier is unable to respond to the incentive of a higher price. Figure 5.22 shows how PES may increase over time.

Thus price elasticity of supply measures the ability of firms to change the quantity supplied in response to a change in price. Factors to consider include:

Figure 5.22: Price elasticity of supply and time

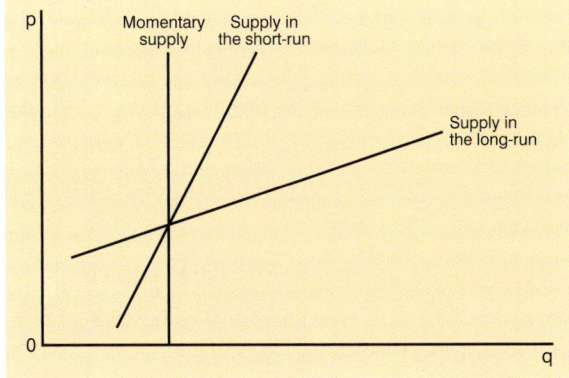

Spare capacity

This refers to slack in the resources of the firm which can be used, if necessary, to meet unexpected increases in demand. Workers may be paid overtime to work longer hours and machinery may be operated more efficiently to boost output. In some cases (and where the reward is particularly high, for example when prices rise dramatically) a firm may bring in extra workers and machinery or outsource production to other plants to ensure output can be increased.

Stocks of raw materials and components

In a similar way to spare capacity above, the ability of the firm to source sufficient raw materials and components will determine PES. The more stocks it holds (or can obtain quickly), the more price elastic supply will be.

Factor of production substitutability

Even when factors of production are fully utilised, a firm may be able to increase output by converting factor use (land, capital, labour, managers) towards the output where price is rising. This may take time, however, and some factors are more flexible in their use than others. In times of crisis, food prices may rise dramatically, in part because agricultural output is mainly determined by annual harvests of crops. These higher prices should, in the long-run, see some landowners move their resources back towards agriculture (instead of, say, biofuels or leisure use), even in economies such as the UK.

Summary questions

1. Why is elasticity a useful concept to economists?
2. Give possible examples of goods (or situations) which may be (i) perfectly price elastic, and (ii) perfectly price inelastic.
3. What are likely examples of inferior goods for (a) low income households in the UK, (b) high income households in the UK, (c) low income households in a developing economy.
4. Goods A and B are substitutes, B and C are complements, C and D are substitutes, and D and A are complements. Identify four goods which fit this situation!
5. 'Firms prefer market conditions where price elasticity of demand is low and price elasticity of supply is high.' Do you agree with this statement? Justify your answer.
6. The price of a brand of mobile phones falls from £300 to £280, resulting in an increase in weekly sales from 900 to 990 phones. Calculate the price elasticity of demand in this instance and also state whether total revenue has risen or fallen as a result of the price cut.
7. An increase in average incomes of 1.5% leads to a 0.5% increase in demand for Good A, a 2% fall in the demand for Good B, and a 4% increase in demand for Good C. Calculate income elasticity of demand for each of these goods, state the type of good they are and give a realistic example of what they could be.
8. The price of cheese increases from £2.00 to £2.40, resulting in a 10% increase in demand for Good F and a 5% fall in demand for Good G. Calculate the cross price elasticity of demand between cheese and each of Good F and Good G, and state the relationship (if any) between the demand for these goods.
9. An increase in the price of pop music festival tickets from £300 to £360 per weekend leads to an increase in the supply from 10,000 to 20,000. Calculate the price elasticity of supply for the festival.
10. In relation to question 9, what factors might limit the ability of the festival organisers to expand their provision of places at the festival even if they believe it would be profitable to do so?

Extension questions

A. Using diagrams, show the producer and consumer incidence of a subsidy where demand is (a) price elastic, and (b) price inelastic.
B. "In the long-run both price elasticity of demand and price elasticity of supply will become elastic." To what extent do you agree with this statement?
C. Research the Cobweb Model and consider its relevance to modern agricultural markets.
D. How useful is the concept of elasticity? List as many examples as possible of its application to the behaviour of each of: (a) households, (b) firms, (c) government.

Chapter 6
Interrelated Markets and Markets in Action

The market mechanism can be used to explain how a change in one market can affect another and this can be applied to many real world contexts. It would be unrealistic to consider a market in isolation as all markets are subject to external influences, some more so than others.

Competitive demand

If two goods are substitutes then they are in competitive demand. If Mercedes become more efficient at producing cars, the supply will increase (S1 to S2) and the equilibrium price will fall (p1 to p2). This will lead to an expansion of demand for Mercedes cars. However the fall in price will lead to a decrease in the demand for BMW (D1 to D2). The extent of the decrease will depend on the value of cross elasticity of demand between the two goods. If it is greater than 1, then they are strong substitutes and demand will fall significantly.

Figure 6.1: Competitive demand – a fall in the price of Mercedes cars leads to a decrease in the demand for BMWs as they are substitutes

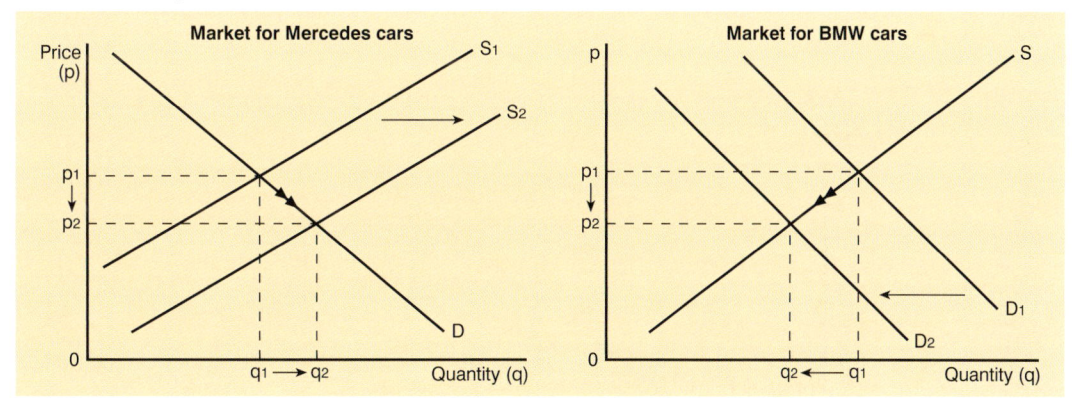

Joint demand

This occurs when two goods are complements. An increase in the supply of mobile phones due to new technology will increase supply (S1 to S2) and lead to a lower equilibrium price (p1 to p2). There is an expansion of demand for mobile phones as a result. This affects the market for ringtones as the increase in quantity demanded of mobile phones leads to an increase in demand for ringtones, because they are complementary goods. This is shown by the demand curve shifting outwards from D1 to D2. The extent of the increase will depend on the cross elasticity of demand between the two goods. If it is less than -1, then they are strong complements and demand will increase significantly.

Mobile phones and ringtones are complementary goods.

Figure 6.2: Joint demand – a fall in the price of mobile phones results in an increase in the demand for ringtones as they are complements

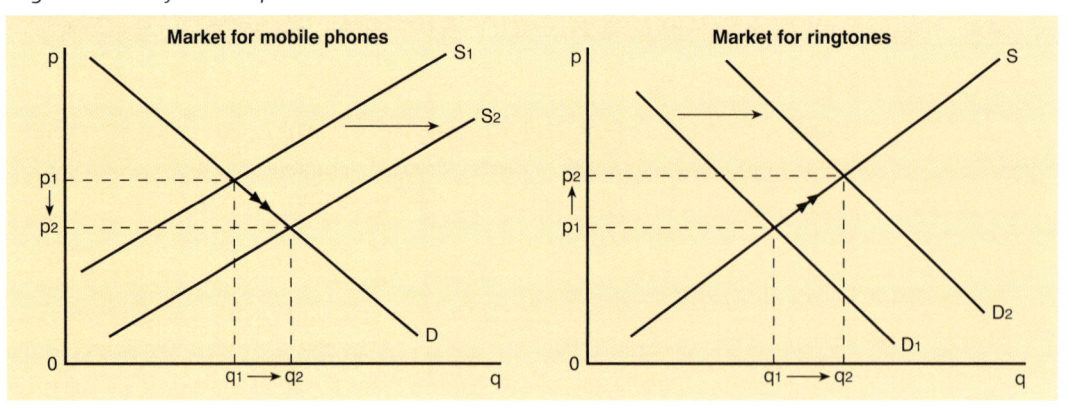

Derived demand

Derived demand describes a market in which a good is demanded not for its own intrinsic use but for another purpose, for example the production of another good. An increase in the demand for cars will lead to an increase in the demand for steel. This is because the demand for steel is derived from the demand for cars as it is required for their production. This is shown by a shift outwards of the demand curve for both markets.

Figure 6.3: Derived demand – an increase in the demand for cars will lead to an increase in the demand for steel

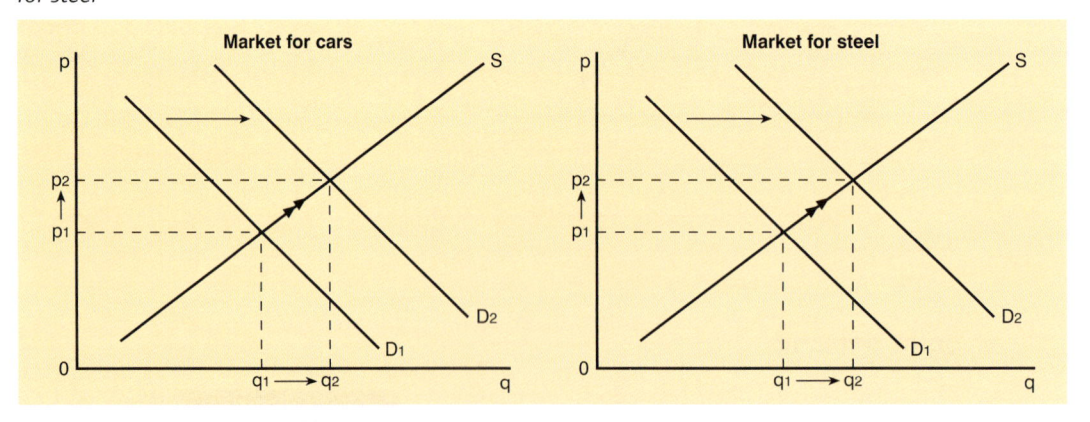

Composite demand

Composite demand exists when a good or service has alternative uses. For example milk can be used for the production of cheese and yoghurt. For a given amount of milk, an increase in the demand for yoghurt (D1 to D2), due to a change in consumer preference for a healthier diet, will lead to an increase in quantity supplied of yoghurt. This implies that there is less milk available for the production of cheese and therefore the supply of cheese falls (S1 to S2).

Composite demand: Milk can be used for the production of cheese and yoghurt.

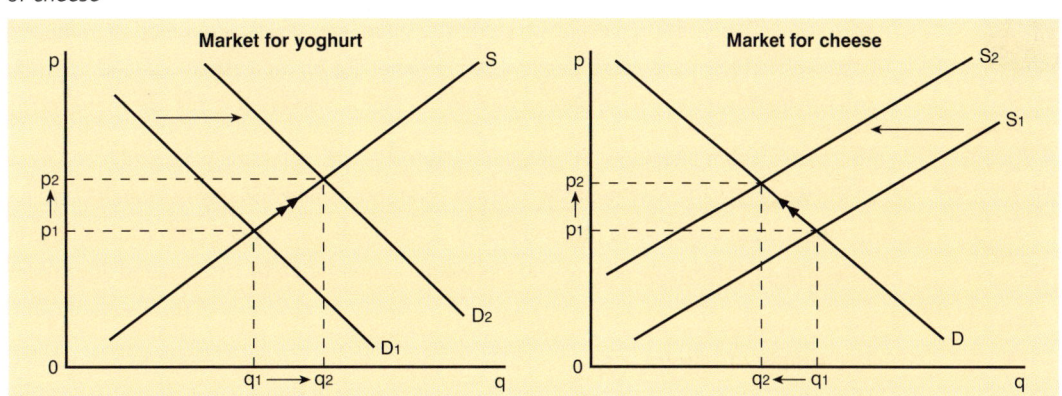

Figure 6.4: Composite demand – an increase in the demand for yoghurt leads to a decrease in the supply of cheese

Joint supply

This occurs when two good are by-products i.e. the production of one product naturally leads to the production of another. Beef and leather is a commonly used example. Figure 6.5 shows that if there is an increase in supply of beef, then this will lead to an increase in supply of leather, with the supply curve shifting outwards in both markets.

Figure 6.5: Joint supply – an increase in the supply of beef results in an increase in the supply of leather

Competitive supply

Competitive supply exists when a firm can produce alternative goods or services from its existing factors of production. An increase in demand for one product will lead to a fall in the supply for the other. For example a farmer may choose between potato or corn production.

Composite supply

Composite supply occurs when the demand for a good or service can be satisfied via different sources. For example the demand for salt can be met by sea salt or salt from mines. An increase in demand for salt is likely to increase the quantity supplied of sea salt and salt from mines, assuming there is no preference for either type of salt.

Applications of the market

The theory of supply and demand and the market mechanism can be applied to the real world to help understand why markets behave differently.

The labour market

Labour is a factor of production (an input into the production process) and therefore if the economy is in an upturn or a boom and production increases, more labour will be required to produce goods and services. Labour therefore has derived demand. More generally, an increase in demand in product markets (goods and services) leads to an increase in demand in factor markets (factors of production).

The price of labour is wages. Of particular interest is the real wage: wages adjusted for inflation, calculated as the wage rate increase minus the rate of inflation. Thus a 5% pay rise when there is 3% inflation in the economy gives a real wage rate increase of 2%. In the same way as the market determines the price of a good using demand and supply, the real wage is determined by the demand and supply of labour.

The supply of labour

The supply of labour is the amount of work that households are willing and able to supply to the labour market at any given real wage rate. It can also be referred to as the labour force or working population and includes all those who are economically active i.e. working, or actively seeking work

Figure 6.6: The labour supply curve

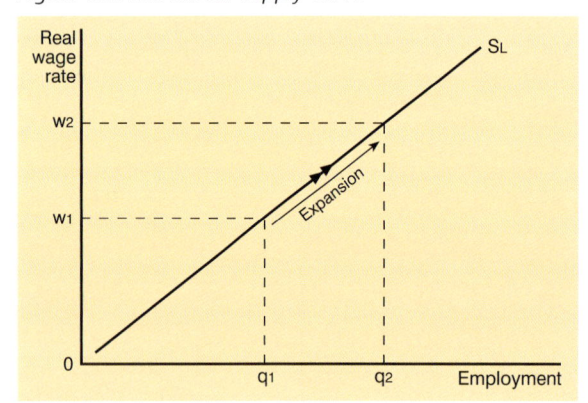

Just as in the product market for goods and services, the supply curve in the labour market is upward sloping, therefore showing a positive relationship between the price of labour (real wage rate) and the quantity of labour (Employment). An increase in the real wage rate will therefore lead to an expansion of the labour supply curve (S_L) by households as shown in Figure 6.6. Note that a change in the real wage rate does not shift the curve but leads to an expansion or contraction of the supply of labour.

There is a positive relationship between the real wage rate and supply of labour because a higher real wage rate means better rewards for labour and an increase in income. This acts as an incentive for households to supply more labour.

The supply of labour can be considered for the whole of the labour market (total of all individual labour supply curves) or in the context of a particular job or industries. Therefore, a higher wage offered by one industry may attract labour from other industries, in addition to those who were previously economically inactive (not included in the labour force).

The demand for labour

The demand for labour is the amount of labour that firms are willing and able to demand at any given wage rate. The demand for labour is a derived demand, because as more goods and services are produced in the economy (an increase in Gross Domestic Product, which measures the output of an economy over a given period of time), more factors of production will be needed to make them, including labour. It is important to remember that firms demand labour, unlike the product market in which consumers demand goods and services.

The labour demand curve is downward sloping as there is an inverse relationship between the real wage rate and the demand for labour. This is because firms demand labour and as wages form part of the costs of production, an increase in the wage rate will increase costs. This will lead profit-maximising firms to reduce the amount of labour that they employ. The higher the wage rate, the less labour firms can afford to hire and vice versa. Also the law of diminishing returns (Chapter 2) explains that in the short-run each additional worker will become less and less productive, assuming the amount of capital (machinery) is

Figure 6.7: The labour demand curve

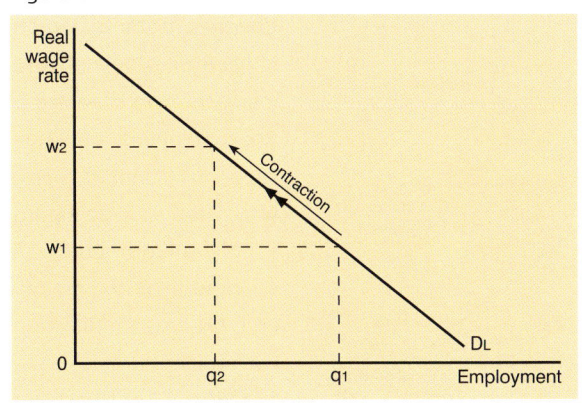

Figure 6.8: Labour market equilibrium

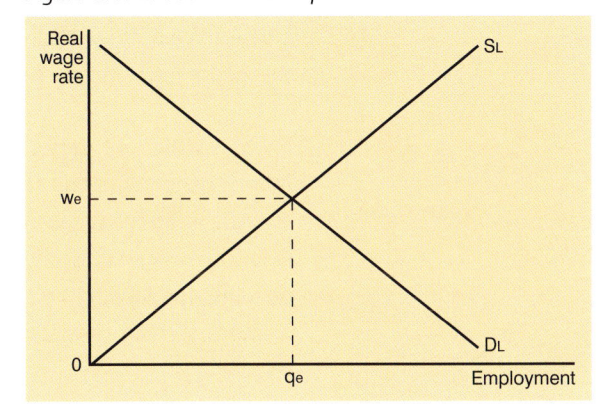

Figure 6.9: An outward shift in the labour supply curve

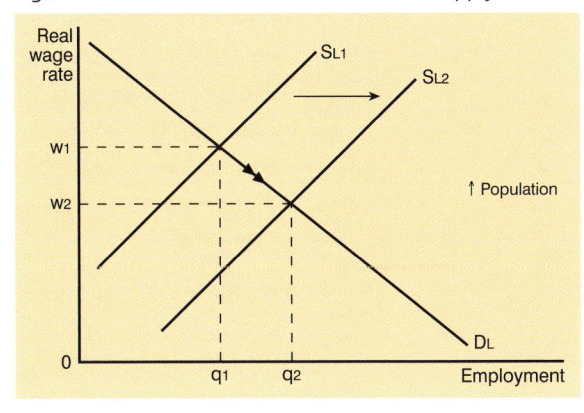

Figure: 6.10: Supply of labour for different occupations

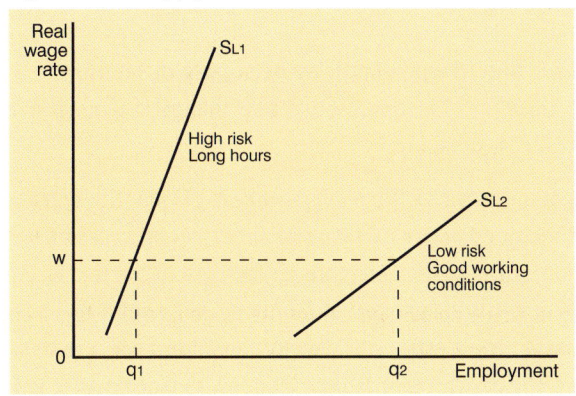

fixed. Therefore as the number of workers increase, firms will only be prepared to pay a wage rate which reflects this reduction in efficiency.

An increase in the real wage rate will lead to a contraction of labour demand curve by firms and vice versa as shown on Figure 6.7.

Labour market equilibrium

The labour market therefore operates in exactly the same way as the product market in theory. Equilibrium is achieved when planned labour demand = planned labour supply and there is no incentive for firms demanding labour or households supplying labour to change their market plans. The equilibrium real wage rate is given by we and the equilibrium quantity of labour (employment) is given by q_e, as shown in Figure 6.8.

Factors which influence the supply of labour other than the real wage rate

In the same way as the product market, an increase or decrease in the following non-price factors will shift the labour supply curve.

Population

An increase in population can lead to an increase in the labour force, increasing the supply of labour at any given wage rate, shown by a shift outwards of the labour supply curve (Figure 6.9). This leads to a fall in the real wage from w1 to w2 and an increase in employment from q1 to q2. As labour is a factor of production, an increase in the supply of labour will enable more goods and services to be produced in the economy. Therefore an increase in population can lead to economic growth.

Non-monetary factors

There are a variety of factors other than the real wage rate that influence the supply of labour. If the level of risk is high or long working hours are required there is likely to be less labour supplied. However if the working conditions of an occupation or industry are favourable, this may give an incentive for labour supply to be higher. This is shown in Figure 6.10.

Figure 6.11: An inward shift in the labour supply curve

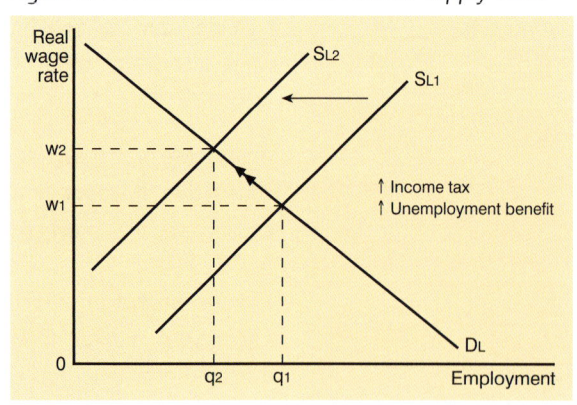

Figure 6.12: An outward shift in the labour demand curve

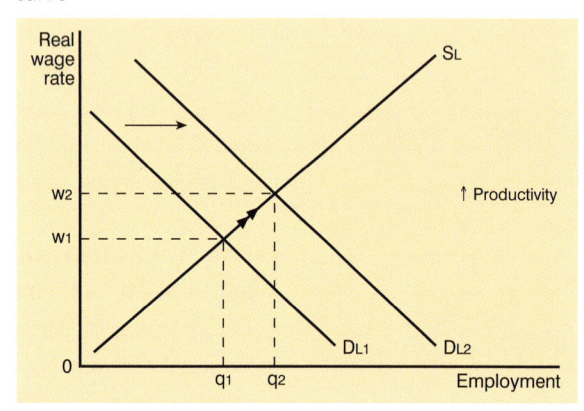

Figure 6.13: An inward shift in the labour demand curve

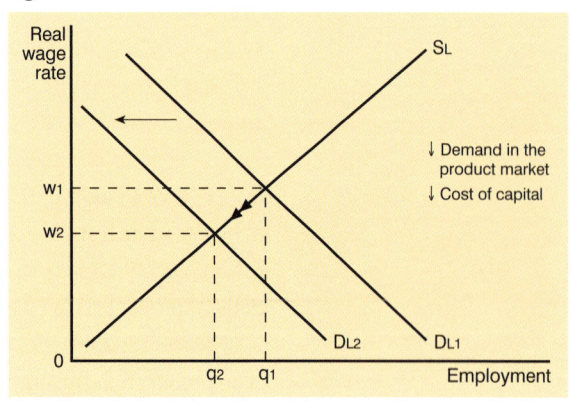

Tax and benefit system

Changes in the tax and benefit system can impact the supply of labour; for example an increase in income tax and an increase in unemployment benefits can reduce the supply of labour as there is less incentive to work, leading to an inward shift in the labour supply curve (Figure 6.11). This results in an increase in the real wage from w1 to w2 and reduces employment from q1 to q2. Governments may try and improve the supply-side of the economy by reducing income tax and unemployment to give the economically inactive an incentive to join the labour force or those that are already part of the labour force an incentive to work more.

Factors which influence the demand for labour other than the real wage rate

An increase in the productivity of labour as a result of education or training will increase demand for labour. This is shown by an outward shift in the labour demand curve (Figure 6.12).

A change in the demand in the product market will influence the labour market. Therefore a fall in the demand for a good or service will decrease the demand for the labour employed to make it, at any given real wage rate, shifting the labour demand curve inwards (Figure 6.13). This leads to a decrease in the real wage rate and a decrease in employment.

The degree of substitutability between labour and capital (machinery) will impact the demand for labour. If the cost of capital decreases and labour can easily be replaced by machinery, then the demand for labour is likely to fall (Figure 6.13). This leads to a decrease in the real wage rate and a decrease in employment.

'Wage' elasticity of demand for and 'Wage' elasticity of supply of labour

The degree to which demand and supply of labour respond to a change in the real wage rate will depend on the elasticity of demand and supply of labour.

The elasticity of demand for labour measures the responsiveness of quantity demanded of labour to a change in the real wage rate. If the good or service requires labour intensive production, then wage costs are likely to be a high proportion of the costs. Therefore an increase in the real wage rates will increase costs significantly, causing the quantity demanded of labour to fall significantly. This means that the demand for labour is wage inelastic. The elasticity of demand for labour will also depend on the ease of substitution of capital for labour. The easier it is to replace labour with machinery (capital), the more wage

Figure 6.14: Increase in demand for labour when labour supply is wage elastic

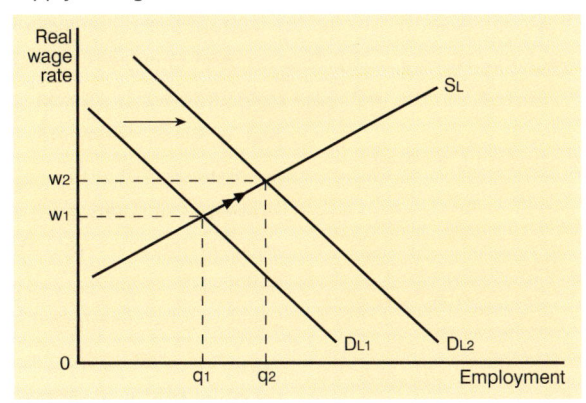

Figure 6.15: Increase in supply of labour when labour demand is wage elastic

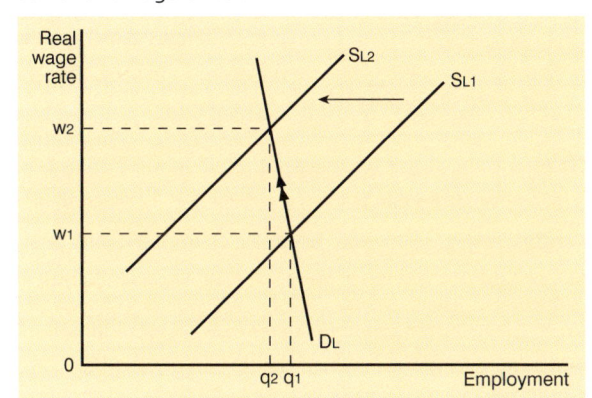

elastic demand is as the labour market can respond quickly to any changes.

The elasticity of supply of labour measures the responsiveness of the supply of labour to a change in the real wage rate. The more skills required, for example in professions such as law, accountancy, medicine and architecture, the more wage inelastic the supply of labour. Even if a higher wage rate is offered it will take time and money for qualifications to be gained and supply of labour to increase significantly.

Therefore the extent to which an increase in the demand for labour has an effect on the real wage rate, depends on the wage elasticity of supply of labour. As Figure 6.14 shows, a wage elastic labour supply curve leads to a proportionally larger percentage increase in employment compared to the percentage rise in the real wage rate. Therefore employment is affected more than the real wage rate.

In the same way, the extent to which a decrease in supply of labour has an effect on the real wage rate depends on the wage elasticity of demand for labour. As Figure 6.15 shows, a wage inelastic labour demand curve leads to a proportionally larger percentage increase in the real wage rate compared to the percentage fall in employment. Therefore the real wage rate is affected more than employment.

The more skills required in professions such as architecture the more wage inelastic the supply of labour.

Immigration

The labour market can be used to analyse the effects of immigration. An increase in immigration leads to an increase in population, which will increase the size of the labour force (*ceteris paribus*), shown by an outward shift of the labour supply curve (Figure 6.16). As a result of immigration, there is an increase in employment from q1 to q2, but a decrease in the real wage from w1 to w2. It may be argued that a fall in real wage for domestic workers is unfair, particularly for lower paid occupations. However, immigration is vital when shortages arise in certain industries, for example healthcare. By increasing employment in the labour market, immigration is also a source of economic growth, increasing the productive potential of the economy and improving the supply side of the economy.

Figure 6.16: The effect of immigration on the labour market

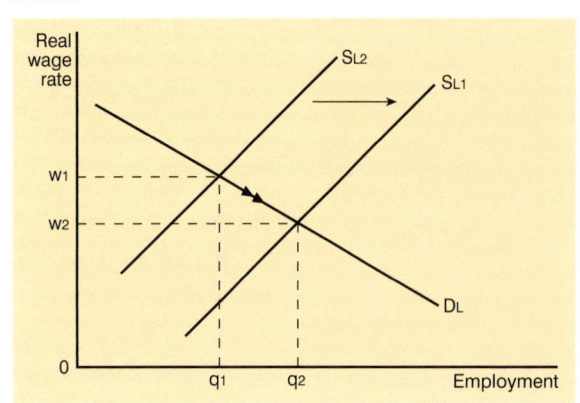

In reality, the impact of immigration depends on the following factors and will vary between different sectors in the economy and occupations.

1. *The wage elasticity of demand for labour* If it is wage elastic, as shown in Figure 6.16, then an increase in supply of labour as a result of immigration can lead to a substantial increase in employment, without reducing the real wage rate significantly. There are, however, many different submarkets within the labour market and occupations will differ in terms of wage elasticities as explained in Chapter 11.

2. *Government policy on immigration varies between political parties* So far in labour market theory, it has been assumed that it is a free market economy, in which there is no government intervention, however in reality governments intervene in the labour market and place restrictions on immigration because in particular localities there is concern over extra numbers placing pressure on schools and social services.

3. *The performance of the economy* During times of recession, a country may be relatively less attractive as a place to work compared to other countries which are performing well, leading to a fall in immigration.

4. *Net migration* When considering the labour market as a whole, net migration should be taken into account. UK workers, for example, may leave to work overseas (outward migration) or overseas workers may come and work in the UK (inward migration). Only if inward migration (immigration) is greater than outward migration, is there likely to be an increase in the overall supply of labour and a resulting fall in real wage rate.

Minimum wage

A government's objective, in theory, is to maximise the welfare of its citizens. If the government believes that the equilibrium real wage is too low and therefore inequitable, then it may set a minimum wage which is above the equilibrium. This ensures that all workers get paid a minimum amount regardless of what type of job they are doing.

The Labour party introduced the National Minimum Wage Rate to the UK in 1999. Since then it has risen each year and in 2014/2015 it was £6.50 per hour for workers who are 21 years and over.

Whilst the minimum wage guarantees a certain standard of living for workers in the UK, it has some disadvantages. One problem with the minimum wage is shown in Figure 6.17. Excess supply of labour or what is known as 'real wage' unemployment will result if the wage is held above the market equilibrium.

The minimum wage reduces the mobility of labour, which is the ability of labour to be put its most effective use (see Chapter 11). As the government intervenes in the market, it over-rides the price mechanism and distorts the functions of price. Trade unions are another cause of imperfection in the labour market, and

Figure 6.17: Labour market imperfections as a result of a minimum wage or trade union collective bargaining

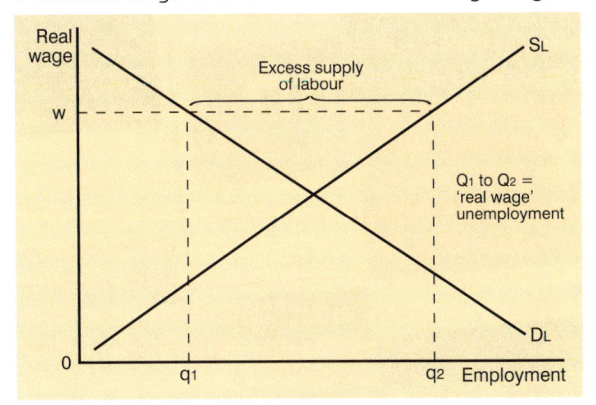

therefore labour immobility. They are organisations which represent workers, often in a particular industry or sector, and use collective bargaining to force the real wage above the equilibrium. This causes the same inefficiencies and unemployment as the minimum wage. The Conservative government under Margaret Thatcher significantly reduced the power of trade unions in order to increase the flexibility of the labour market.

The housing market

The UK has a much higher proportion of homeowners than similar economies in Europe. Therefore the housing market has an extremely important influence on the economy and vice versa.

The demand for housing

Rising standards of living as a result of strong economic performance has increased the demand for houses. Therefore the income elasticity of demand for housing is positive i.e. houses are normal goods.

Most homeowners have a mortgage, which is a loan from the bank specifically for buying property and is another example of derived demand. Consumers will need to pay back interest to the bank on top of the original loan. Therefore any changes in interest rates will affect the majority of the UK population. A decrease in the interest rate may increase the demand for housing and vice versa.

Speculation can also affect the housing market. The demand for housing is very much connected to confidence in the economy. If the economy is doing well and individuals have job security, then taking out a large mortgage is not such a big risk. However, a downturn in the economy may lead to a downturn in the housing market as banks and consumers become less prepared to lend and borrow respectively (for example in the Credit Crisis of 2008).

The supply of housing

The supply of housing is price inelastic, at least in the short-run and medium-term, as it takes time for the market to respond to increased demand due to long time lags between deciding to build more houses and their completion. Limited availability of land may also restrict supply, particularly in terms of regulations which restrict land use, such as green belt areas.

Figure 6.18: The housing market – an increase in demand will lead to a significant increase in house prices due to a relatively price inelastic supply

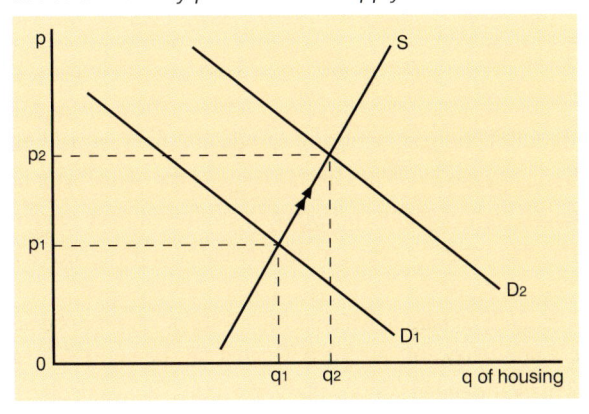

Figure 6.18 shows the effect of these demand and supply factors. The fact that supply is price inelastic means that house prices increase significantly if the economy is strong and there is increasing demand. This may prevent many first time buyers from getting on the 'housing ladder'. A fall in confidence in the economy however, may lead not only to a decrease in demand but the significant possibility of a large fall in house prices.

It is important to also consider the rental market for housing. This often works in the opposite direction to the homebuyers market

If there is a fall in confidence some consumers may put off their decision to buy and rent instead.

and the two are to some extent substitutes in the UK. If there is a fall in confidence then some consumers may put off their decision to buy and rent instead, which increases the demand for rental property. The opposite will happen when the economy picks up again.

Whilst the theory of supply and demand can be useful for analysing the housing market, it is important to consider that the overall housing market can be divided into many submarkets depending on geographical location. (A submarket is simply when a market can be subdivided into specific, identifiable markets.) Therefore factors influencing one submarket may not impact another submarket in the same way. For example, there is much higher demand for properties in London as it is the capital city and is also home to the 'city' where a large proportion of the financial service sector is based. This market will differ greatly from rural Scotland for example where house prices will be lower due to less demand and there will be far less market transactions due to the location.

Also the housing market should be considered at both local and national levels. The local market for housing may be influenced heavily by the location of good schools whereas change in the base rate of interest will impact the housing market nationally.

Commodities markets

Commodities markets are examples of markets on a global scale. Commodities are unprocessed or partially processed goods such as oil, precious metals, beef or grain. These goods often suffer from price fluctuations as a result of speculation on the stock market and particularly volatile demand and supply conditions. The market for oil is a good example of this.

Demand for oil

Oil is a necessity which is required for the production of goods and for fuel. It is therefore a derived demand and is price inelastic. In recent years there has been a surge in the demand for oil as countries such as China and India have experienced high economic growth and as a result have required more oil. Global demand was already high, but this has added to pressure on producers to meet such a high demand.

Supply of oil

Oil is a fossil fuel and therefore a non renewable resource. Once it has been used, it cannot be replaced. The amount of supply to the oil market depends on a variety of factors. For example, changes in the cost

Figure 6.19: The oil market – price stabilisation by OPEC

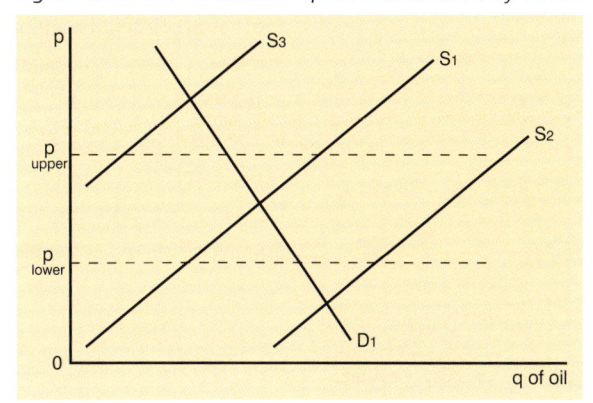

of drilling and refining oil, wars destroying oil fields and the discovery of new oil sites can all add volatility to the market price as supply will increase or decrease accordingly. The volatility is made even worse by speculators who trade on future prices of oil in order to make money. In very simple terms, oil will be purchased if it is believed that there will be an increase in price in the future and sold if it is believed that the price is going to fall.

All of the above gives some justification for the presence of OPEC which was set up to control fluctuations in prices. It achieves this by restricting supply when the price of oil is too low (below the lower price boundary) and releasing the supply of oil, when the price oil is too high (above the upper price boundary). This is shown in Figure 6.19.

However, this system relies on the oil producing countries having enough oil to release when prices are too high. If supply is restricted beyond their control, then they will not be able to reduce prices. Also OPEC can contribute to price volatility by such interventions in the market, particularly as demand is price inelastic.

The price mechanism through the functions of price ensures that scarce resources are allocated efficiently. Therefore as oil becomes increasingly scarce as a result of massive global demand and falling supply, higher prices can only be expected by consumers. This may in time lead to alternative fuels being developed which are perhaps more environmentally friendly and consumers demanding less oil and switching to cheaper and 'cleaner' substitutes.

The market mechanism helps us to understand how a change in demand or supply affect the market, however in a market such as commodities, the frequency of changes are so vast that it makes it impossible for consumer or producers to have perfect information, particularly as these markets are on a global scale. The model is limited by its static nature i.e. it considers the market at a point in time, assuming everything else is held constant (ceteris paribus). However, in reality the commodities market is extremely dynamic (changes over time). This explains the high degree of speculation which occurs in these types of markets.

Financial markets

The financial market is also an example of a market that has submarkets; for example, it can be split into markets for loans, credit cards, mortgages, pensions, online savings etc.

The money market can be explained using the theory of supply and demand. The price of money is given by the real interest rate (r) i.e. interest rate which has been adjusted for inflation. The demand for money is simply the demand for cash or very liquid assets, such as current accounts which can be easily converted into cash. The money demand curve (MD) is downward sloping because the lower the interest rate, the cheaper it is to borrow money from the banks and there is less incentive to save, therefore the quantity demanded increases. The supply of money is the amount of money circulating in the economy. As UK money supply is controlled by the Monetary Policy Committee at the Bank of England, it means that regardless of an increase or decrease in real interest rates, it will remain constant at a point in time. The money supply curve (MS) is therefore perfectly inelastic as it is not responsive to a change in the price of money (real interest rate).

If the Bank of England increases the money supply, this is shown by a shift outwards in the vertical money supply curve as shown in Figure 6.20. An increase in money supply from q_1 to q_2 will lead to a fall in the real interest rate from r_1 to r_2.

Figure 6.20: An increase in the money supply

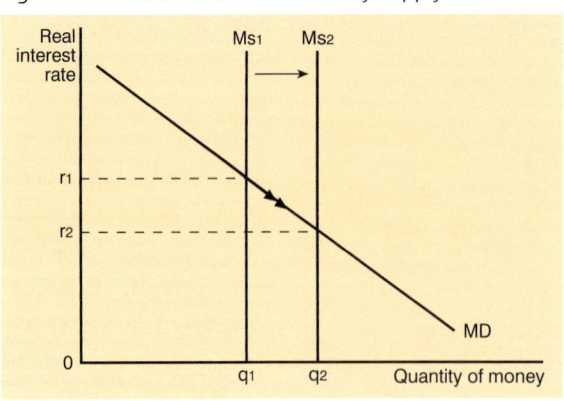

However, whilst the model provides a useful tool for predicting the impact of the Bank of England's decision to change money supply, in reality there are many different submarkets in the financial sector and whilst generally it is expected that interest rates will follow in the same direction, the degree to which they do may differ and some may not at all.

Agricultural markets

Agricultural markets often suffer from price fluctuations as there are external shocks such as weather and disease which can affect harvests or production. The government may intervene to stabilise the market price by using a buffer stock scheme. This ensures that producers get enough income each year and therefore have an incentive to keep supplying to the market even after a bad harvest. Consumers also benefit from steady prices.

Figure 6.21: Buffer stock scheme

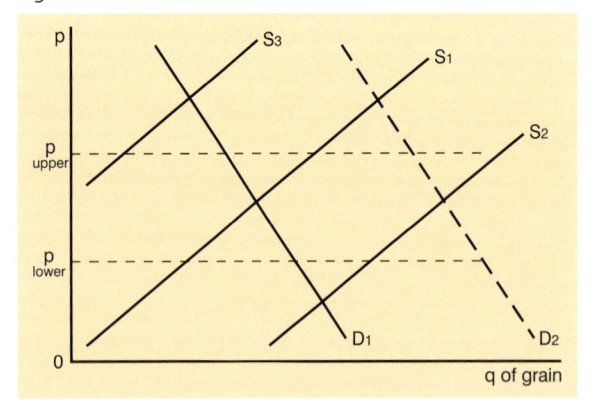

A buffer stock scheme requires price boundaries to be set, with an upper or lower limit. The government will not intervene if the equilibrium price remains within these boundaries. However, taking the example of grain, if there is a good harvest then supply will increase (S1 to S2 on Figure 6.21). If supply increases too much, the new equilibrium price may fall below the lower price limit. The government intervenes by buying grain, thereby increasing demand (D1 to D2) until the equilibrium price increases to a point where it is back within its boundaries. The government will then store any grain that it has bought which will act as a buffer to price volatility. If, in the next year there is a bad harvest, the supply of grain decreases (S1 to S3). If supply decreases too far then the price will be higher than the upper limit. The government intervenes by selling the grain that it has in storage until supply increases (S3 to S1) to the point that the equilibrium price has fallen back within its boundaries.

Buffer stock schemes can be used in other volatile markets such as commodities. For example, a commonly known scheme is for natural rubber and is run by the International Natural Rubber Organisation. Another example is the International Tin Council's buffer stock scheme to control the price of tin. However, with increased demand for substitutes such as aluminium, the demand for tin fell so drastically that the buffer stock scheme had to be abandoned in 1985 due to lack of funds.

Buffer stock schemes offer benefits to both consumers and producers in the form of price stability. However there are several disadvantages. They have high start-up and administration costs and the government needs enough resources to always be in a position to buy a surplus of the good, as necessary. There is also the cost of storage and the fact that food may perish over time, potentially leading to waste. The scheme relies heavily on there not being too many bad or good harvests in succession, otherwise there will not be enough supply to sell, or money to buy, the good if required. Producers may also catch on to the fact that if they keep overproducing, then they will always have a dedicated customer, the government!

Evaluation of the theory of supply and demand/the price mechanism/ the market mechanism

Economic theory provides a benchmark for reality. It helps to explain how markets work and predicts how changes can affect the market. This helps all economic agents to make their market plans, for example firms can make forecasts and budgets.

However, a number of assumptions are made to simplify the model and do not necessarily reflect reality.

Firstly, it is assumed that consumers and producers are rational and that their sole motivation is to maximise utility and profit, respectively. It is also assumed that individuals' preferences are fixed. However consumers' demand may be influenced by powerful factors, such as word of mouth, peer pressure, habitual or addictive behaviour which will cause consumers to demand more at a higher price than would be deemed rational by economic theory.

Secondly, it is assumed that consumers and producers have perfect information. In reality, this is not the case. Whilst the internet has helped significantly to keep track of price changes, consumers and producers may lack the time or ability to gain all possible information on a good or service when making their market plans.

It is also assumed that producers have no influence on the market price due to a large number of firms existing in the market, all producing identical (homogenous) products. However there are many markets in which there are few, large dominant firms, which enables them to increase the price in order to maximise profit (Chapter 7).

In terms of the labour market, economic theory assumes there are no dominant buyers of labour (monopsony) and an individual firm has no influence on the wage rate. This again does not reflect reality as firms exploit their power by offering lower than competitive wage rates. Labour however can respond by collective bargaining and forming trade unions, in order to increase the wage rate.

Summary questions

1. Explain why currency is an example of derived demand.
2. Give *two* other examples of derived demand.
3. Explain why land is an example of composite demand.
4. Give *two* other examples of composite demand.
5. Is an increase in demand for beer good or bad news for marmite lovers? Explain your answer using diagrams and identify how the markets are interrelated.
6. With reference to all four elasticity measures in Chapter 5, explain the importance of elasticities to the UK housing market.
7. Explain how buffer stock schemes such as the Common Agricultural Policy can be used to stabilise food prices.
8. Explain why buffer stock schemes may give producers an incentive to supply too much to the market.

Extension questions

A. The National Minimum Wage was introduced in the UK in 1998 and unemployment actually fell significantly over the next eight years. Evaluate the impact of the minimum wage and other factors on UK employment and unemployment.
B. What are the advantages and disadvantages of reducing the power of trade unions?
C. Evaluate the impact of abolishing the European Union's Common Agricultural Policy on low income households in economies such as the UK.

Part Two: Markets and Government Failure

Chapter 7
Introduction to Market Failure

Types of economy

The basic economic problem is what to produce, how to produce it and who to produce it for. An economy is a system which attempts to allocate scarce resources in such a way as to provide the combination of goods which maximises social welfare, or the sum of all individual's utility.

There are three main types of economy: free market economies, command economies and mixed economies.

Free market economies leave the allocation of factors of production to market forces. The prices of all goods and services are determined by supply and demand. The main problems with a free market economy are the provision of goods and services which may create serious social problems (such as drugs, weapons and pollution) and the inequalities which may arise as some members of society find it difficult or impossible to earn a wage at which they can live comfortably.

Command economies use state control to allocate resources. This can, in theory, lead to greater equality and reduce or even remove production and consumption of dangerous goods and services. The government decides what is produced and may use non-price factors, such as greatest need or waiting lists, to decide which households are allowed which goods and services. The main problems with a command, or centrally-planned economy, are a lack of incentives to both workers and entrepreneurs (unless wages are linked to productivity, or some degree of 'profit' is allowed) and the bulky administrative mechanism of trying to control and allocate vast resources and goods to meet the needs of millions of people.

The mixed economy allows a compromise between the two extremes of free markets and central planning, and in reality most economies in the world are mixed to some extent. In a mixed economy, the government leaves most markets to market forces, allowing demand and supply to influence prices and create incentives for entrepreneurs to innovate and compete; but in some markets a value judgement is made that partial or total intervention is required, most typically in the markets for education, healthcare, transport, law and order and emergency services. The reason for intervention in these markets is market failure.

Market failure: addressing the balance

Market failure arises when the equilibrium price and output levels in a market are socially undesirable and/or create inefficiency. The market price of iPods and holidays are rarely controversial; these are non-essential goods and, if a household cannot afford them, this is viewed as a natural symptom of market forces. Some households earn more than others because they have different levels of human capital, usually due to differing levels of skills, qualifications and experience. This creates different levels of spending power which can be either accepted ('life is like that') or changed (by developing personal human capital, or voting for a government with a more distributive policy).

But most societies believe that some goods are special: they should be available to all members of society, whether rich or poor. The lowest income households tend to be young, old or ill, and these vulnerable groups may not have the income or information necessary to spend money on goods which will benefit both themselves and society in the long-run: education, preventative medicine and a healthy lifestyle, and transport to work and school. Thus the government may step in (to varying degrees in different countries) to try to ensure that everyone has a basic standard of living and level of opportunity to make the most of their talents and contribute to society.

Governments may provide goods such as transport and education.

Identifying market failure is difficult and controversial because it involves making a value judgement about what is 'good' and what is 'bad' for an economy. What is obvious is that if the production and consumption of all goods and services were left to market forces, society would not necessarily benefit. This may be because of the nature of the good itself (the optimal quantity of certain hard drugs and weapons may be deemed to be zero) or due to the market conditions in an industry: the relative levels of demand and supply which mean that some goods are overprovided and over-consumed whereas others are underprovided and under-consumed.

The following chapters outline typical market failures, and the content of each is summarised below.

Chapter 8 looks at monopoly power: when there are a small number of dominant suppliers in a market, it is likely that prices may rise and quality fall. The abuse of monopoly power is a big issue in a world economy where vast multinational companies dominate markets such as fast food, software and branded clothing. Monopoly suppliers are usually regarded as productively and allocatively inefficient but there are exceptions, and the debate on the relative *dynamic* efficiency of monopolies and more competitive markets is of particular importance.

Chapter 9 looks at externalities: the spillover effects resulting from the production and consumption of certain goods. Externalities are not considered by the producer or consumer unless a third party (typically a pressure group or the government) makes them do so. Externalities may result in missing markets, where without some form of government intervention a good is under or over produced, or even not produced at all. The economics of externalities is very interesting, not least because it is linked to major topical issues such as road congestion and climate change.

Chapter 10 also examines missing markets: those goods and services which may not be produced at all under free market conditions (public goods) and those which would be traded at socially undesirable quantities, either because the benefits they bring to society (merit goods) or the problems they cause (demerit goods) are not fully accounted for by market forces.

This chapter will also look at the issue of information failure. Many economic models have traditionally assumed that economic agents – households, firms and governments – have perfect information and they base their decisions on this perfect knowledge of both the present and the future. Behavioural economics contests this viewpoint and can therefore shed light on situations where economic agents appear to be behaving irrationally. Information gaps, or imperfect knowledge, can lead to market failure, for example in the case of monopolistic firms which can exploit their dominant position, or when individuals might consume harmful goods because the full extent of the damage this causes to themselves or others is not fully known.

Chapter 11 looks at two further causes of market failure: factor immobility and inequality. Economists often disagree about the distinction between causes and consequences of market failure and these arguments will be explored throughout the second half of this book, and in this chapter in particular. Much recent economic research is taking place in the area of information, and market failure can often arise due to poor quality information.

Chapter 12 ends the book by reviewing the policies available to governments to tackle and correct market failure. Thus the mixed economy can, in theory, provide an efficient allocation of resources in all markets and social welfare can be maximised against the constraint of limited available factors of production. However, government failure may also arise; this is where government action fails to increase (or actually decreases) social welfare. The problems of imperfect information, unintended consequences and Public Choice Theory will be explored in detail here.

Summary questions

[You should return to these questions after reading all of the book and think about how your answers may have changed.]

1. What problems may arise in a totally free market economy?
2. What problems may arise in a command/centrally planned economy?
3. What is meant by the term market failure?
4. Give three examples of market failure in actual markets. Which of the categories of market failure do you think these are?
5. Why may the actions of governments not always result in improvements in social welfare?

Extension questions

A. Consider the market for public transport. List as many reasons as possible why quick and cheap public transport is important in an economy.

B. What do we mean by social welfare? Research the concept of Pareto efficiency and consider how this is linked to productive and allocative efficiency.

C. Research 'creative destruction', a term coined by Joseph Schumpeter. How does this idea inform the debate on the merits of competition versus monopoly power?

D. Choose three countries; to what extent are they a free market economy (and what data would help you make this decision)?

Chapter 8
Monopoly Power and Competition

There are two definitions of a monopoly: theoretically, a monopoly is defined as a market structure in which there is only one firm in the industry. However it is also useful to know the working definition of a monopoly: a firm with at least 25% market share. Royal Mail is an example of a monopoly in the UK, although it has been gradually opened up to the benefits of competition in recent years.

Characteristics of a monopoly

Barriers to entry

A monopoly exists when there is only one firm (or a dominant firm) in the market and monopoly power tends to persist because of high barriers to entry which prevent other firms from entering the market. There are different types of barriers to entry.

High set-up costs are often a deterrent to new firms. Whilst it is possible for an existing firm to operate on a large scale which enables it to pay off any loans, a new firm is often operating on a small scale and is unable to compete.

Many large firms build up **brand loyalty**. This may be achieved by spending large amounts on marketing and advertising campaigns. A firm considering entering the market would be unlikely to afford to compete, unless it is a company like Virgin which is already a brand name and can afford to diversify into different markets such as air travel, soft drinks, cosmetics etc.

Some monopolists may engage in **anti-competitive practices** to deliberately restrict or remove competitors from the market. This is usually regarded as one of the most harmful consequences of monopoly power.

There are potential benefits to consumers of barriers to entry as they can help monopolies to protect their profit, which may then be invested in research and development. This may improve the quality of their products in the long-run.

Price makers

Barriers to entry prevent competition and therefore allow a monopoly to charge the price that it chooses. It is therefore known as a price maker in that it chooses where, on the industry demand curve, to operate. In order to maximise profit, theory states that a monopoly will charge a higher price than the free market equilibrium price under a competitive market. As a result of this, the demand curve dictates that a higher price will lead to a lower quantity demanded in the market.

Perfect and imperfect competition

In economics there are various forms of market structure shown in Figure 8.1. At the opposite end of the spectrum to monopoly is *perfect competition*, which is the 'benchmark' in terms of achieving economic efficiency. The key characteristics of this market structure is that there are many firms in the industry which are all producing identical products (known as a homogenous products) and have no monopoly power to influence the overall market price. Perfectly competitive firms are called 'price takers' and it is the market as a whole, made up of many firms, which dictates the price via market demand and supply. If a firm tried to charge a higher price then consumers would be able to buy identical products from another firm at a lower price. If a firm tried to charge a lower price, then it would not be able to earn enough profit to remain in the industry. It is important to note that perfectly competitive firms have no barriers to entry to prevent other firms entering the industry and taking their share of the industry profit.

Figure 8.1: Spectrum of market structures

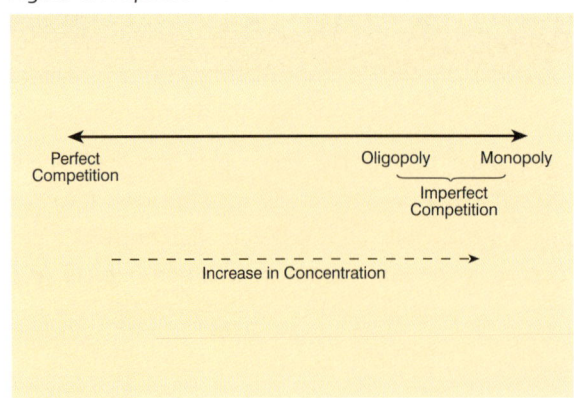

```
←───────────────────────────────→
Perfect                  Oligopoly   Monopoly
Competition
                            Imperfect
                           Competition

- - - - - - - - - - - - - - - - - →
         Increase in Concentration
```

Competitive firms lead to economic efficiency. Firstly, the existence of competition gives firms an incentive to drive down costs in order to maximise profit. A perfectly competitive firm is therefore referred to as **productively efficient** as it produces at the lowest average cost. Average cost is simply calculated by total cost divided by output. One way of illustrating productive efficiency is using the production possibility frontier. All points on the curve are productively efficient as output is maximised with a given number of inputs and therefore, in monetary terms, average cost is minimised.

The second type of efficiency achieved is **allocative efficiency** which in simple terms means that consumer welfare is maximised. It is commonly thought of in terms of consumers benefiting from a low price, but it can also consider whether the market is providing what consumers desire, whether it be quality of a good or choice. Allocative efficiency is achieved under perfect competition as price taking firms charge the free market equilibrium price which maximises consumer surplus as seen in Chapter 4.

In reality there are very few industries which come close to perfect competition: the foreign exchange market and agricultural markets are common examples. Perfect competition should therefore be regarded as a benchmark which achieves an efficient allocation of resources and is useful to measure other market structures against.

All other forms of market structure are known as imperfect competition and have some degree of monopoly power, allowing some or all firms in the industry to be 'price makers'. Monopoly is at the extreme end of the spectrum with the most monopoly power, however it is also useful to be aware of an oligopoly which is more realistic and applicable to the real world. This occurs when there are a few dominant firms in the industry which have monopoly power. The working definition of monopoly (over 25% market share) is of relevance here as this is usually the case for dominant firms in an oligopolistic market. There are many examples of oligopolies such as in the mobile phone, airline and music industries.

Barriers to entry may prevent other firms from entering the market.

A useful term when looking at different market structures is **concentration**. The lower the level of competition in a market, the more 'concentrated' the market becomes. The concentration ratio measures the dominance of the largest firms in the industry. For example, a four firm ratio of 70% means that the four largest firms in the industry have, in total, 70% of the total market share.

The main differences between perfectly competitive markets and those exhibiting oligopolistic or monopoly power are summarised below:

Perfect Competition	**Imperfect Competition**
Firm is a 'price-taker' with little or no ability to determine prices: market price is set by demand and supply across the whole industry	Firm is a 'price-maker' with some influence over the prices set: market price is set by demand and supply for the products of this firm only, and may differ from those of competitor firms
Profits will tend to be low, especially in the long-run*	Profits will probably be higher
Easy entry and exit from the industry	Significant barriers to entry and exit
Product is similar or identical to those supplied by competitor firms	Significant product differentiation, supported by strong branding and often high levels of spending on marketing

*Economists use a technical definition to distinguish between the long-run and the short-run.

In the **short-run**, the quantity of at least one factor of production employed by a firm is fixed in quantity, for example a farm may have a given level of land, alongside which the farmer can vary their use of labour and physical capital.

In the **long-run**, all factors of production are variable. Using the example above, in the long-run the farmer can increase (or decrease) the amount of land used by the business.

Price and non-price competition

Price is a key determinant of demand, but firms compete with their competitors on other variables too. Price is an important consideration when consumers decide what to buy and which supplier to buy from, but their choices will also be influenced by factors such as:

- quality of the product
- brand image and reputation
- marketing campaigns
- brand loyalty
- quality of customer service
- speed of delivery
- quality of after care
- warranties and guarantees

Thus firms may be able to charge a higher price if customers know (or at least perceive) that the wider benefits, or utility, derived from the consumption of the good or service is sufficiently positive to outweigh this.

Monopolies and market failure

Imperfectly competitive markets such as monopolies may lead to market failure as they result in an inefficient allocation of resources.

Figure 8.2: Monopoly and productive inefficiency

Productive inefficiency
Compared to a perfectly competitive firm (c*q*), a monopoly does not have the same incentive to drive down its costs of production. Therefore a monopoly may be described as productively inefficient as it does not produce at its lowest average cost (c1q1) as shown in Figure 8.2.

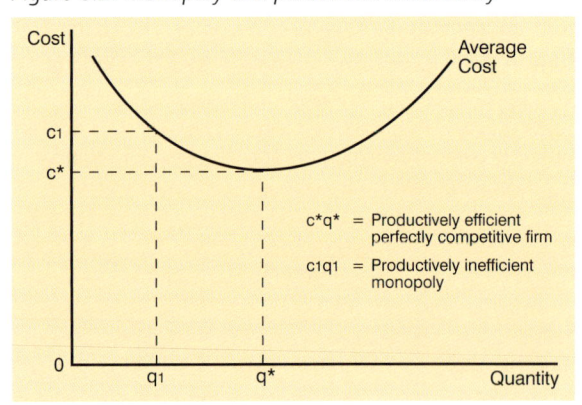

Figure 8.3: The effect of a monopoly on consumer surplus leading to allocative inefficiency

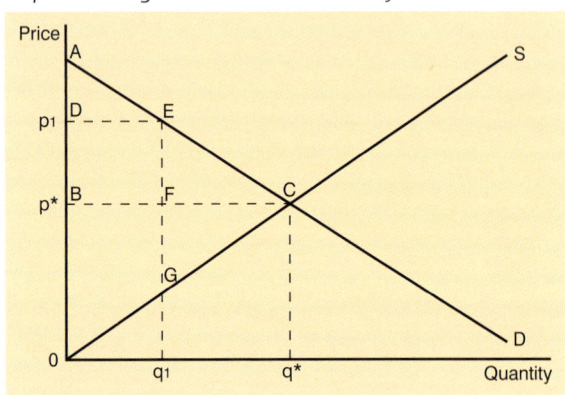

Allocative inefficiency
Figure 8.3 shows the effect of a monopoly or a firm with monopoly power charging a higher price. As previously mentioned, any firm which has a degree of monopoly power is a price maker. Profit-maximising monopolies will therefore decide to charge a higher price (p1) than competitive firms (p*). This means that the quantity of the good or service supplied will be restricted from q* to q1, as the law of demand still holds. A perfectly competitive firm in contrast is a price taker and will charge the free market equilibrium price and output (p*q*) which maximises consumer surplus (ABC) and is therefore allocatively efficient.

Reminder: consumer surplus is the difference between the price that consumers are willing to pay (represented by the demand curve) and how much they actually pay. Producer surplus is the difference between the price at which producers are willing to supply a good or service to the market and the price which they actually receive.

The higher price under monopoly conditions reduces consumer surplus from ABC to ADE. Therefore allocative inefficiency occurs as consumer welfare is no longer maximised. However, monopolies benefit from the transfer of consumer surplus to producer surplus, which is represented by the area DEFB. There is still an area which is unaccounted for, ECG, which is called the deadweight loss to society. Due to a fall in the quantity of the good in the market, consumers are losing out. Fewer consumers are now able to afford the higher monopoly price, supporting the argument that monopolies lead to a misallocation of resources and therefore market failure.

So far, monopolies have been compared to perfect competition in the context of market failure, but it is also important to consider oligopolies. An oligopoly is characterised by a few dominant firms in the industry which leads to interdependency in terms of their price strategies. For example, an airline such as BA will consider the possible price strategies of its competitors for similar flights before setting its own prices.

This interdependence may lead oligopolies either to **collude**, for example by fixing prices and forming cartels (which are illegal in the UK) or **compete**, leading to 'price wars'. If firms collude in some way, this is likely to be damaging to the consumer as it often leads to higher prices. Dominant firms benefit from higher profits than if they competed against each other. Thus the cartel effectively acts as a monopoly and therefore leads to market failure. If firms compete, this may benefit consumers as firms cut prices and try to win consumer loyalty. It should be noted, however, that this is a short-run pricing strategy as price wars may eventually lead to the elimination of firms' profit and is therefore undesirable to the firms (if not to consumers!).

Advantages of monopolies

So far monopolies have been presented in rather a bad light. The fact that firms with monopoly power are often allowed to exist must mean there are some benefits to these price makers.

Dynamic efficiency

So far productive and allocative efficiencies have been mentioned, which are both classed as static efficiency: efficiency at a point in time. In contrast, dynamic efficiency is efficiency over time. This may be achieved by the invention of new goods and services or innovation in technology or supply techniques. One argument is that monopolies with high barriers to entry are able to protect their monopoly profit and can afford to carry out research and development which will improve dynamic efficiency. Microsoft, for example, is able to use its huge profits to develop better versions of Windows. Competitive firms may not have the resources or the incentive to carry out research and development if their ideas are not protected in any way and information is shared in the market. One could therefore argue that the quality of goods and services will be superior under a monopoly than in a competitive market and this will increase the welfare of consumers over time. Others would argue that competition is necessary for invention and innovation.

Economies of scale

One aspect that monopolies may have in their favour is size. Barriers to entry help to prevent competition and maintain a monopoly's market share. The ability to operate on a large scale brings several benefits in terms of cost. Economies of scale occur when an increase in output leads to a fall in long-run average cost from q_1 to q_2, as shown in Figure 8.4. Whereas in the short-run at least one factor of production is held constant, for example it is not usually possible to suddenly acquire more land, it is assumed that, in the long-run, all factors of production are variable and therefore the scale of a firm can be increased. It can therefore be argued that a monopoly may be able to achieve lower average costs than a productively efficient perfectly competitive firm as it operates on a much larger scale. Monopolies may be more productively efficient than perfectly competitive firms in some cases.

Figure 8.4: Economies and Diseconomies of scale

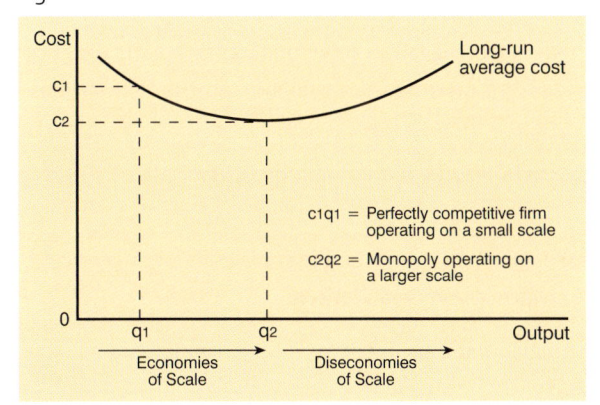

There are several types of economies of scale, all of which lead to falling average costs as a result of increases in the scale of production.

Managerial economies: a large firm has the resources available to hire specialist managers who are more productive than in a small firm in which one person may be running the whole business. Large firms often have finance, marketing and sales departments for example, and greater specialisation should lead to higher quality output and lower average costs.

Financial economies: banks lend money to firms in return for interest payments on top of the initial amount to be paid back. A large, established firm with strong brand loyalty carries less risk to the bank compared to a small firm entering a new market. Therefore large firms are likely to be able to negotiate cheaper loans with lower interest payments.

Purchasing economies: due to its size, a monopoly may have bargaining power over its suppliers and therefore reduce its costs of production considerably. It also has the ability to buy large quantities at a time, which leads to discounts.

Technical economies: it may only be financially viable for a company of a certain size to operate in a market if the machinery or technology required is very expensive. In other words, the output needs to be large enough for the average cost of production to fall to an affordable level.

Figure 8.4 also shows that if a firm gets too large then long-run average costs may start to increase. This is known as diseconomies of scale and can be due to lack of coordination, motivation and communication resulting from greater organisational complexity and the types of management issues more common in larger firms. This is therefore a limitation to the argument of economies of scale which may or may not apply depending on the industry.

Diseconomies of scale

If economies of scale are the benefits a firm enjoys from increasing its size, diseconomies of scale are the costs created by expansion.

Motivation can be a problem in large organisations, where workers may feel their efforts are not valued as highly as in a small firm, or when it is difficult to link individual effort to annual profit or other measures of business success.

Motivation may be a problem in large organisations.

Management costs may also rise as more levels of monitoring and support are added to cope with the larger workforce. This can also lead to slower decision-making and the firm may lose out on profitable ventures as a result.

Bureaucracy and compliance costs may be higher in larger organisations if they are regulated more strictly than smaller firms.

Complex, multinational businesses must also manage differences in language, culture and time zones which can also increase average costs in these organisations.

It is important to note that economies and diseconomies of scale can arise in all large firms and not just those enjoying monopoly power.

Natural monopolies

One advantage of monopoly power is the possible existence of natural monopolies. This occurs when there are natural barriers to entry which prevent others from entering the market, and thus there is only room for one firm in the market. A good example of this would be water companies which have natural monopolies in their local areas. This is because the cost of creating competition by duplicating pipeline (or other distribution) networks would be both expensive and inefficient, thus reducing social welfare. Note that a natural monopoly may still use its market power to raise prices above the perfectly competitive level – see the section below for possible government responses to this.

Abuse of monopoly power and government intervention

A government will intervene in a market if the existence of monopoly power is deemed to lead to a misallocation of resources and therefore market failure.

The main method used is via command and control. Regulation can restrict monopoly power if it is detrimental to consumers.

The Competition and Markets Authority (CMA) is responsible for ensuring markets operate competitively and fairly in the UK. The main areas of the CMA's work are summarised below.

1. **Merger control** – the CMA has the power to prohibit mergers which will lead to a 'substantial lessening of competition'. They key concern is not market share, but the ease of entry into the industry after the merger. If the CMA believes the merger will harm consumers and competitor firms unreasonably, mergers can be blocked.

2. **Market investigations** can be undertaken where there appears to be a lack of competition in a market. The CMA has strong powers to impose behavioural conditions on firms where there is proved to be 'adverse effects on competition' and there may even be a legal requirement to sell off part of a business where this is the case. Examples of recent investigations in the UK include retail ('high street') banking and energy markets.

3. **Economic regulators** act as a substitute for competition in industries where there are high concentration ratios, often due to natural monopoly. These regulators can impose limits on the ability of the monopolist to raise prices or reduce the quality of their products or customer service.

4. **Abuse of dominant position** occurs when a monopoly acts to reduce the competition it faces, for example by driving competitors out of the market ('predatory pricing'), tying the supply of one good to another (e.g. bundling of Windows Media Player within the Microsoft Windows platform), or blocking access to facilities needed by all firms in a market to survive (e.g. airport landing slots).

5. **Collusive agreements**, or the forming of cartels, allows a group of firms (none of which may have significant market share) to collectively form a monopoly. These agreements are illegal, and along with abuse of dominant position can be punished by significant fines are payment of compensation to affected parties.

In all cases where a firm, market or sector is investigated, analysis may hinge on the PQRS combination: impacts on price, quality, range and service.

Limitations of regulation
Regulation is only effective if it is enforceable and the administration costs do not outweigh the overall benefits of government intervention. If firms believe that no action is going to be taken, then there is no incentive for them to change their behaviour. Further limitations are discussed in Chapter 12, in particular regulatory capture and unintended consequences.

Nationalisation
Governments may decide the best way to control monopolies is to own them and provide the goods and services directly to households. After the Second World War many firms were nationalised in order to rebuild the country. Many utilities such as water, gas, electricity and telecommunications were also owned by the government (note that these are natural monopolies **and** essential goods for consumers). The argument for government ownership would be that the government is able to control prices and ensure, if necessary, that all households can afford basic necessities. This may improve allocative efficiency. However, a government-run monopoly faces no competition and therefore may become productively and dynamically inefficient.

Privatisation
The Thatcher government in the 1980s carried out a wave of privatisation which opened up the majority of nationalised industries to competition. By breaking up previous monopolies, it was hoped that firms would compete against each other and drive down both costs and prices to increase efficiency. Whilst costs may have been driven down by privatisation, the extent to which consumers have really benefited from lower prices is debatable. As utilities are often natural monopolies, competition is limited and therefore a large degree of monopoly power and therefore allocative inefficiency still remains.

Figure 8.5: Maximum price in a monopoly market

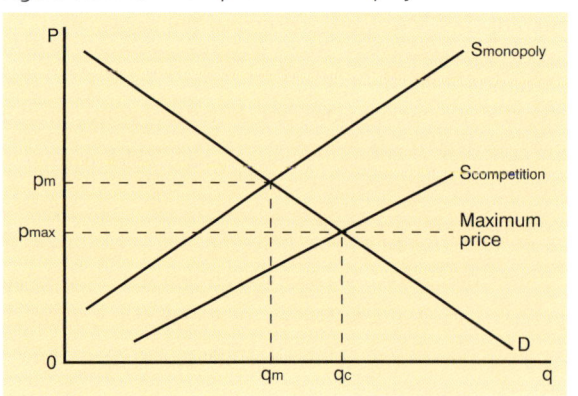

Price controls

The government may decide to impose maximum prices on the output of monopolists. Figure 8.5 shows a market where a maximum price of p_{max} has been imposed to prevent a monopolist abusing their monopoly power to push up prices. The maximum price is set at the same level as that prevailing under competitive conditions.

Taxation

In some circumstances the government may tax monopoly profits in an attempt to transfer welfare back from the monopolist to the consumer (albeit indirectly).

One problem with this policy is the impact it may have on dynamic efficiency: it has been argued earlier that some monopolists use profits to invest and innovate.

Defining 'the market'

A final, but important consideration when determining market structure and the potential for the abuse of monopoly power is what exactly is meant by the market for a good. Local or even time-specific monopolies may exist when there is inelastic price elasticity of demand, for example in a cinema where popcorn prices can be high, or in a nightclub where prices will be considerably more expensive than in a nearby bar, and in turn even higher than from an off licence.

A major determinant of whether the abuse of monopoly power is important is also the nature of the good itself. There is significant market concentration in the world market for diamond supply, resulting in very expensive engagement rings. However, this monopoly in what is a luxury market might be viewed as considerably less important than high prices leading to high profits in the supply of electricity, water or

Local monopolies may exist when there is inelastic price elasticity of demand, for example in a nightclub where prices will be considerably more expensive than in a nearby bar.

Summary questions

1. Define both monopoly and monopoly power.

2. What are the main characteristics of a monopoly?

4. What does a concentrated market mean and how is it measured?

5. The market share of each of the largest supermarkets in the UK is shown below (data: December 2014):

Tesco	29.1%	Cooperative	6.1%
Asda	16.7%	Waitrose	5.0%
Sainsbury's	16.5%	Aldi	4.9%
Morrisons	11.2%	Lidl	3.7%

Calculate the 5-firm concentration ratio for this industry.

6. What are the implications of this competition data for the UK supermarket industry?

7. Explain, with reference to three measures of efficiency, why monopolies may lead to market failure?

8. Explain possible advantages of allowing monopoly power to persist in certain markets.

9. Apple enjoys considerable market power in the market for smartphones and tablets. Is this beneficial or harmful to consumers?

10. How might a firm in a monopoly position avoid suffering from diseconomies of scale? And is it possible for competitive firms to benefit from economies of scale?

Extension questions

A. What factors will influence whether a monopoly is productively efficient or inefficient?

B. Investigate the EU Commission's case against Microsoft for anticompetitive behaviour. Is current policy justified?

C. Research the concept of X-inefficiency. How does this differ from productive efficiency and how may the level of competition in a market determine X-efficiency?

D. Research Joseph Schumpeter's concept of 'creative destruction'. What are the implications of this theory for the established monopolies of the 21st century, such as Microsoft, Google or Pepsico?

Chapter 9
Externalities

Economic activity takes place when a good or service is produced, provided and consumed. A market is any mechanism which allows a buyer and seller to agree on a price for the good and service and allow exchange to take place.

However, the activities of buyers (or consumers) and sellers (or suppliers/producers) may have wider effects on the community and environment. These spillover effects, or external costs or benefits, are known as externalities. In considering the impact of economic activity on social welfare, it is important to examine both the private costs and benefits (those affecting consumers and producers) and the external costs and benefits (those affecting third parties).

Social Benefits = Private Benefits + External Benefits

Social Costs = Private Costs + External Costs

Net Social Benefit (or overall impact on social welfare) = Social Benefits − Social Costs

Externalities can exist in consumption or production or both at the same time and are a form of market failure.

Negative externalities in production

Negative externalities in production occur when a firm causes a negative spillover effect (external cost) on third parties as a result of the production of a good or service. For example, a factory may cause pollution. Pollution can harm economic welfare by eroding the quality and cleanliness of air and water, creating noise, or degrading the aesthetic environment.

If the good or service is left to the free market, the market fails to take into account the impact of the pollution as a result of production.

Demand can also be referred to as marginal private benefit (MPB). Consumers buy the goods and services which maximise their utility, or satisfaction, and this has a positive impact on social welfare. Producers base their decision on the private costs of production: the payments necessary for the factors of production required to supply the good. The marginal private cost curve is effectively the supply curve for the good, i.e. the price required to produce one more unit of output.

Figure 9.1 shows the supply curve (S1) which represents the decisions made by profit maximising producers who only consider their own private costs (the payments required for the factors of production to produce the good or service). The intersection with the demand curve gives the free market equilibrium price (pm) and quantity (qm). However, social costs include the private costs **and** external costs. This will **increase** costs of production and the supply curve will shift inwards (S2) so that the socially optimum (socially efficient) level of output is achieved. The socially optimum output takes into account the full cost to society, including the costs to any third parties caused by the negative externalities. Therefore, if left to the free market, a negative externality in production, such as pollution, leads to an over-

Figure 9.1: Negative externalities in production using demand and supply analysis

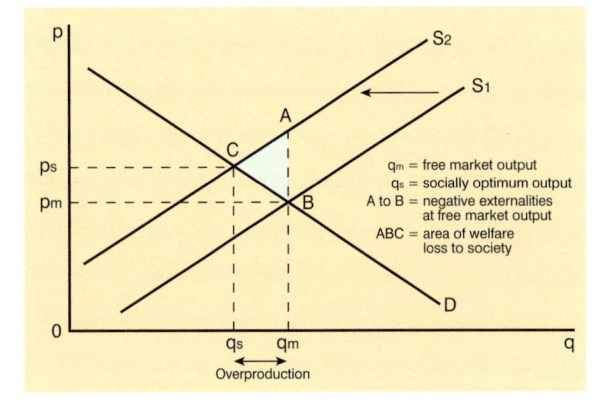

qm = free market output
qs = socially optimum output
A to B = negative externalities at free market output
ABC = area of welfare loss to society

Overproduction

production of the good or service. This is shown by the difference between the free market output (q_m) and the socially optimum output (q_s).

This can also be explained in **marginal** terms. Marginal in economics means additional, so for example marginal private cost can be defined as the cost to a firm or individual of producing an additional unit of output. The equations can be adapted as follows:

Marginal Social Benefits = Marginal Private Benefits + Marginal External Benefits

Marginal Social Costs = Marginal Private Costs + Marginal External Costs

The marginal private cost curve is equivalent to the supply curve for the good. Demand can also be referred to as marginal private benefits (MPB). Consumers buy the goods and services which maximise utility and this has a positive impact on social welfare. However, where negative externalities in production exist, the marginal social costs (MSC) are greater than the marginal private costs (MPC) as shown in Figure 9.2.

The free market output (q_m) occurs where MPC = MPB

The socially optimum output (q_s) occurs where MSC = MSB

In this example, it is assumed that there are **no externalities in consumption** and therefore MPB = MSB.

Market failure occurs because the Marginal Social Costs are greater than the Marginal Social Benefits at the free market output, leading to an overproduction in the free market (q_m is greater than q_s).

Figure 9.2: Negative externalities in production using marginal analysis

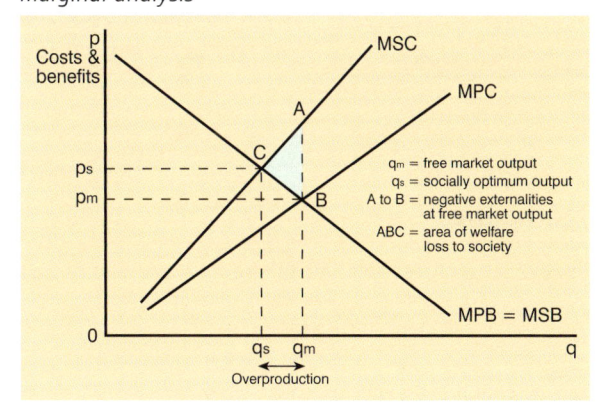

At q_m, the external cost is given by the vertical distance AB in both Figure 9.1 and 9.2. The shaded region ABC, represents the range of output where marginal social costs exceed marginal social benefits due to the negative externalities in production and is an area of welfare loss to society.

Note that market failure does not occur because Marginal Social Costs are greater than Marginal Private Costs, but rather **Marginal Social Benefits are not equal to Marginal Social Costs at the free market output**, due to the existence of negative externalities in production.

Negative externalities in consumption

Negative externalities in consumption occur when an individual's consumption of a good or service has a negative spillover effect on other economic agents or third parties. They can exist on a more localised scale, for example anti-social behaviour in a street late at night as a result of alcohol consumption.

As the externality is in consumption, the demand curve is affected. Utility maximising consumers will only consider the private benefits of drinking alcohol and not the full cost to society, which includes the negative external benefits (external costs) as a result of their consumption. This leads to a free market output of q_m. However if the demand curve takes into account the negative externality of anti-social behaviour, for example noise pollution or an increase in crime, then it would shift inwards D1 to D2, giving the social optimum output of q_s as shown in Figure 9.3.

The free market output is greater than the socially optimum output leading to an overconsumption of alcohol.

Figure 9.3: Negative externalities in consumption using supply and demand analysis

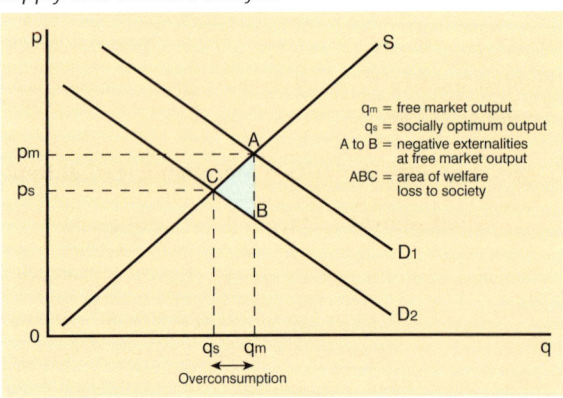

Figure 9.4: Negative externalities in consumption using marginal analysis

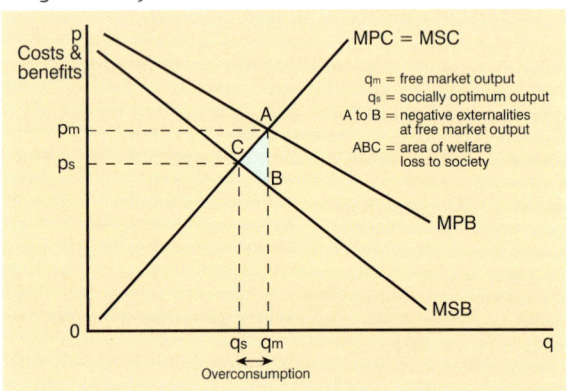

In marginal terms Figure 9.4 shows that in this example the marginal social benefits are less that the marginal private benefits (due to the **negative** external benefits caused by excessive alcohol consumption). Remember that the free market output is determined where MPB = MPC and the socially optimum output is determined where MSC = MSB. It is also assumed that there are no externalities in production. Therefore market failure occurs as marginal social costs are greater than marginal social benefits at the free market output, leading to an overconsumption of alcohol in the free market (q_m is greater than q_s).

The vertical distance AB in both Figure 9.3 and 9.4 represents the negative externality in consumption at the free market output. The triangle ABC represents the range of output at which the marginal social costs are greater than the marginal social benefits due to the negative externalities in consumption. This is an area of welfare loss to society.

Policies to tackle negative externalities

Governments may choose to intervene to correct market failure with the aim of achieving the socially optimal allocation of resources.

Bans

Goods which create negative externalities in either consumption or production are seen as 'bad' for society unless the level of output is moved to the socially optimal level. One possible policy is to ban the good altogether. However, as tempting as it may be to assume that shifting production and consumption to zero will maximise social welfare, in reality this is rarely the case. Figure 9.5 shows the impact on welfare of banning a good such as cigarettes or unleaded petrol. The free market level of output is q_m which creates external costs equivalent to the area surrounded by the boundary points ABC. However, banning the good altogether removes a range of output where private benefits actually exceed social costs, i.e. output between zero and q_s. Thus the ban actually removes the net social benefit marked as the region CEF.

Figure 9.5: Impact of a ban on social welfare

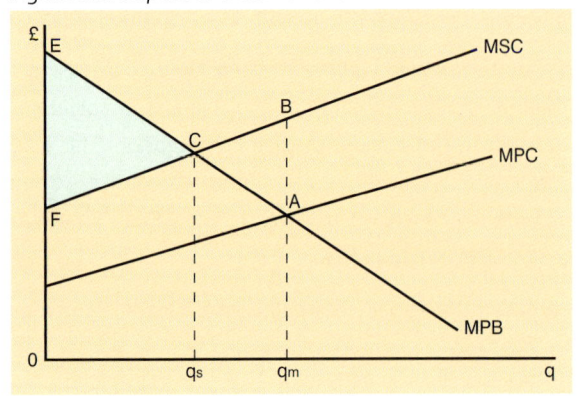

Is a ban ever justified? The answer is yes. Figure 9.6 shows a market for a good where the socially optimal level of output is zero: there is no output level where private benefits exceed social costs and in this case a ban is justified.

Figure 9.6: Ban is justified: all levels of output have MSC > MPB

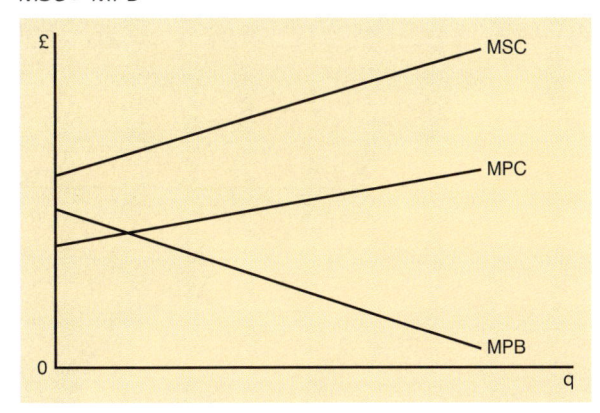

Figure 9.7: Internalising the externality through indirect taxation

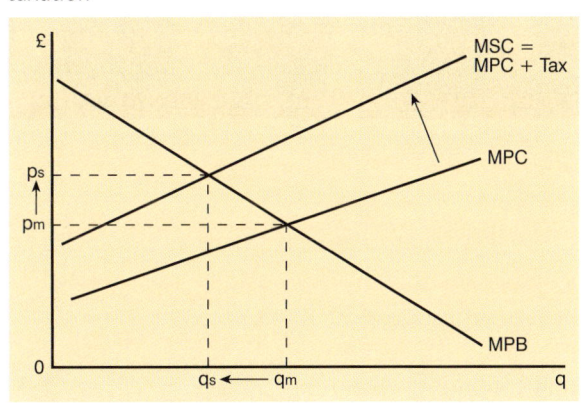

Taxes

Taxing goods which create negative externalities is very common and such taxes are called, variously, green taxes, sin taxes and Pigou taxes (after the English economist Arthur Pigou). It is shown in Figure 9.6 that an outright ban may actually harm social welfare even where negative externalities exist. The imposition of an indirect tax on the supply of a good shifts the supply curve (or social cost curve) to the left, limiting output and pushing up price. Thus, if the tax is set at a level equal to the external cost per unit, the supply curve becomes the marginal social cost rather than the marginal private cost curve. Thus the market equilibrium after the tax becomes the socially optimal output. This is shown on Figure 9.7.

This process is called internalising the externality: the tax imposes an additional cost to the producer (some or all of which may be passed onto the consumer) equal to the external cost to society.

Subsidising alternatives

Taxing a 'bad' will reduce quantity demanded to some extent, depending on the price elasticity of demand of the good. An alternative is to reduce demand for the 'bad' by subsidising alternatives, for example biofuels research and production to reduce the demand for petrol, or subsidising nicotine substitutes to help smokers quit cigarettes.

Compulsory consumption

A more drastic approach may be to make certain alternatives compulsory, such as enforced recycling to limit waste sent to landfill sites. In some areas of the UK this has been controversial as large fines have been imposed on households committing apparently minor errors of refuse sorting! As with any such policy, monitoring and legal enforcement may be necessary – and also expensive. Chapter 12 looks at government failures such as those potentially arising from policies such as this in some detail.

Regulation

The production and consumption of goods which incur external costs on society are often regulated by government legislation. For example, alcohol and cigarettes are regulated by age limits and can only be sold in certain outlets and (in the case of alcohol) at certain times.

Extending property rights

Absence of property rights is linked to externalities and can be viewed by economists as a form of market failure. Property rights are the entitlement of an individual to legal ownership. However if they do not exist, in the case of the atmosphere, then negative externalities may arise as there is no owner to demand compensation or charge for its use. However by extending property rights to, for example, clean air and peace and quiet, polluters can be made liable for the external costs they create. For example, if a smoker

One solution to limiting carbon dioxide emissions is to use a scheme of permit trading.

at a bus stop was forced to pay compensation to anyone breathing in their smoke both the quantity of cigarettes consumed would be lower, and third parties would be compensated for their discomfort (providing property rights can be fully enforced).

Cap and trade/Pollution permit trading

Global warming is seen by many as one of the most pressing problems to face the world. One solution to limiting carbon dioxide emissions (on a local, national or global level) is to use a scheme of permit trading, also known as cap and trade. This sets a quota (a maximum level) on polluting activities such as air travel or heavy industry.

Such a scheme involves a maximum limit being placed on emissions. Permits are then distributed between all polluters, with permission granted to trade permits as desired. In theory, such a scheme provides an incentive to reduce emissions (and develop cleaner technologies) without limiting output (and therefore economic growth and development) in industries and economies which are unable to afford clean technologies. The free market for permits would, in theory, require minimal monitoring: low polluting industries would sell unused permits to high polluting industries and, in the long-run, the total level of emissions could be reduced as cleaner energy sources are developed.

Figure 9.8: Market for pollution permits

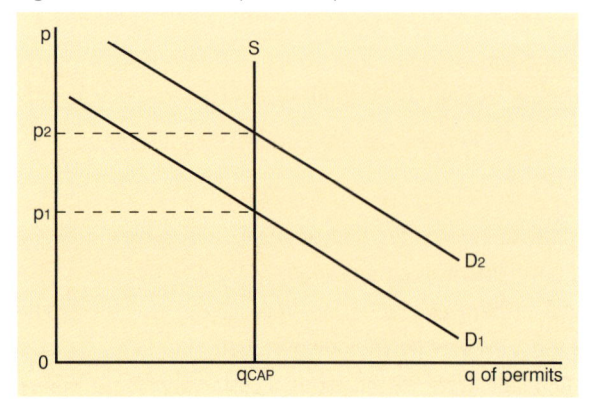

Figure 9.8 shows the market for pollution permits, in which the supply curve is price inelastic as it is determined by the set quota (q_{CAP}) imposed by the government. If more permits are demanded (D_1 to D_2) as firms' production leads to higher levels of pollution, then this will increase the price (p_1 to p_2), giving an incentive to firms holding permits to reduce their emissions so that they can profit from selling their permits.

A permit scheme – in which, effectively, a market for pollution is established – requires

agreement on the maximum level and **enforcement** to ensure all emissions are included within the system. It combines **market-based** and **command and control** methods of government intervention (Chapter 12), as a market for permits is established which allows the price mechanism to allocate resources but also requires enforcement to ensure that polluters are not exceeding their limit.

Personal carbon allowances

Road pricing

Roads are an interesting example in which there are negative externalities in terms of congestion as an individual's car use impacts other motorists as time is wasted queuing in traffic jams. However, this only occurs during peak times i.e. the rush hour.

One approach to internalising this negative externality is a tax charged to motorists who use the certain roads at peak times. The London Congestion Charge is an example of this, in which motorists entering the Congestion zone (roads in central London) need to pay a specified amount (£11.50 per day in 2015) to use the roads within the zone between 07:00 and 18:00 on week days.

This method requires technology to be able to identify cars entering the zone and check whether or not a driver has paid for the use of the road. Enforcement is therefore required and fines given where the congestion charge has not been paid.

Whilst this type of government intervention is successful at charging only those who cause the negative externalities ('the polluter pays principle'), it still may lead to government failures (Chapter 12), such as high administration costs, difficulty setting the correct amount of tax per unit to internalise the externality so that the socially optimum output is achieved and unintended consequences, such as local businesses suffering from a fall in revenue as a result of the congestion charge.

Positive externalities in consumption

Figure 9.9: Positive externalities in consumption using supply and demand analysis

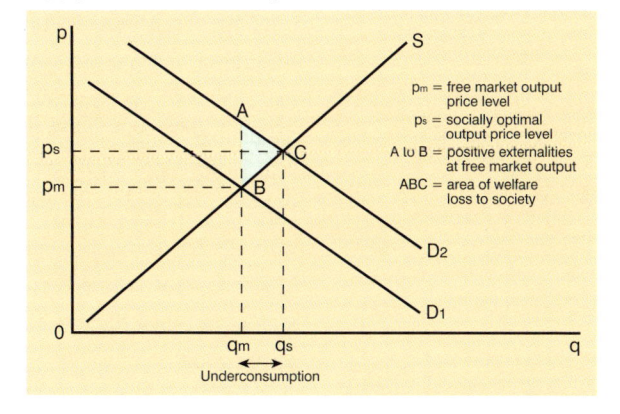

Positive externalities in consumption occur when an individual's consumption leads to a positive spillover effect on society. For example measles vaccinations have a positive effect not only to the individual (private benefits) but also reduce risk of others contracting measles and increase the health of the population (external benefits). Figure 9.9 shows how this can be represented using supply and demand analysis. As the externality is in consumption, it is the demand curve which shifts outwards when the full benefits to society are considered (social benefits). Remember Social Benefits = Private Benefits + External Benefits. The socially optimum output (q_s) is therefore greater than the free market output (q_m) leading to an underconsumption (underprovision) of a good such as vaccinations.

In marginal terms, Figure 9.10 shows that the marginal social benefits are greater than the marginal private benefits, due to the existence of marginal external benefits. Assuming there are no externalities in production, the free market output q_m is given where MPC = MPB and the socially optimum output q_s is given where MSC = MSB. The free market equilibrium (q_m) is less than the socially optimum output (q_s) leading to an underconsumption of the good. In other words there is an underallocation of resources to a market for a good which provides positive externalities in consumption.

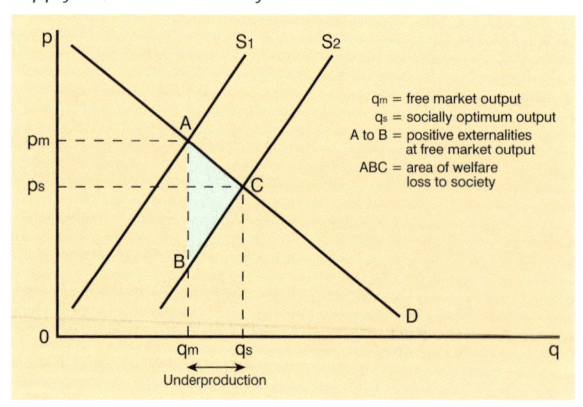

Figure 9.10: Positive externalities in consumption using marginal analysis

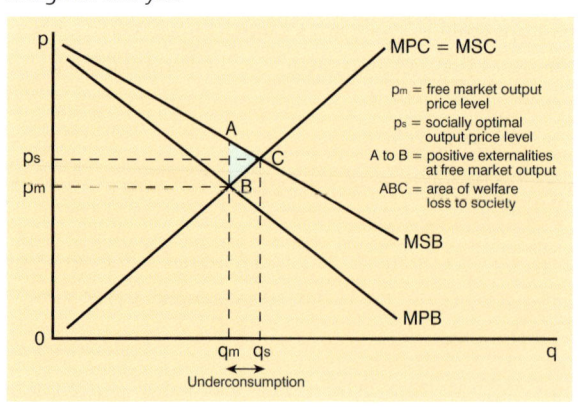

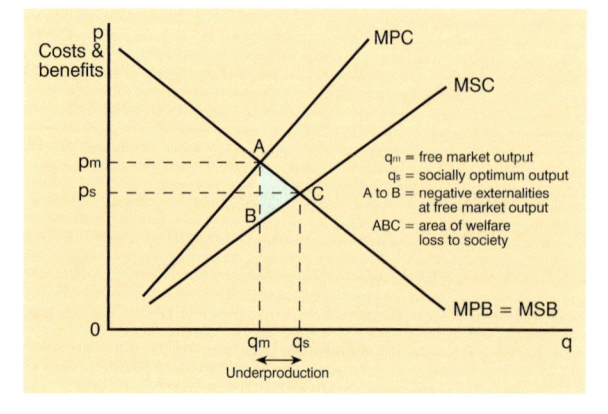

In both diagrams, the positive externality in consumption at the free market output is shown by the vertical distance AB. The triangle ABC represents the range of output where marginal social benefits exceed marginal social costs due to the positive externalities in consumption and is an area of welfare loss to society. Note that this triangle can also be referred to as **potential** welfare gain if output was increased from the free market output (q_m) to the socially optimum amount (q_s). It is called a 'loss' because the benefits are not actually being obtained due to underconsumption.

Positive externalities in production

Positive externalities in production occur when production by a firm leads to positive spillover effects on third parties. For example firm's production can involve training labour and providing skills, which can then have benefits to others when labour transfers to other firms and can share knowledge and skills.

Externalities in production will always affect the supply curve. The supply curve (S_1) as shown in Figure 9.11 only takes into account private costs, however social costs include external costs, which in this case are negative as the positive externality effectively lowers the cost of production, shown by a shift outwards of the supply curve (S_1 to S_2). As a result, the free market output (q_m) is greater than the socially output (q_s) and there is an underproduction (underprovision) of the good or service.

Figure 9.11: Positive externalities in production using supply and demand analysis

In marginal terms, Figure 9.12 shows that marginal social costs are less than the marginal private cost. This is because there are **negative** marginal external costs (Positive externalities in production). Assuming there are no externalities in consumption, (Marginal Private Benefits = Marginal Social Benefits), the free market output (at MPB = MPC) is less than the socially optimum output (at MSB = MSC). Market failure therefore exists in the market because there is an underproduction of the good.

Figure 9.12: Positive externalities in production using marginal analysis

In both Figure 9.11 and 9.12, the positive externality in production is shown by vertical distance AB at the free market output (q_m) and the triangle ABC represents the range of output where marginal social benefits exceed marginal social costs. This is an area of welfare loss to society and can also be viewed as a **potential** welfare gain if output is increased from the free market output (q_m) to the socially optimum output (q_s).

Policies to tackle positive externalities

Figure 9.13: Subsidising a good with positive externalities

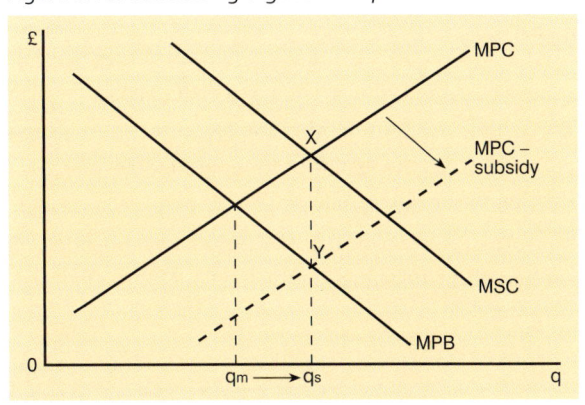

Subsidies

The government can increase the incentive to supply goods with positive externalities through the use of subsidies. Producers are paid a subsidy of XY per unit (see Figure 9.13), i.e. the subsidy sufficient to shift MPC outwards and create an equilibrium output of q_s. This internalises the externality by including the full social benefits (rather than just private benefits) in the market price of the good.

Regulation and compulsory consumption

Just as the government can aim to deter the demand and supply of goods which carry external costs, regulation can also be used to increase production and consumption of goods with external benefits. Examples include compulsory minimum school leaving ages and compulsory motor insurance. These policies aims to increase the demand for the good.

Property rights

Multiple externalities

Both consumption and production externalities can occur simultaneously. The motor car industry, for example, may lead to negative externalities in production from car manufacturers emitting pollution from their factories and negative externalities in consumption from drivers creating pollution and congestion when they use the finished goods.

Figure 9.14: Multiple externalities in the market for cars

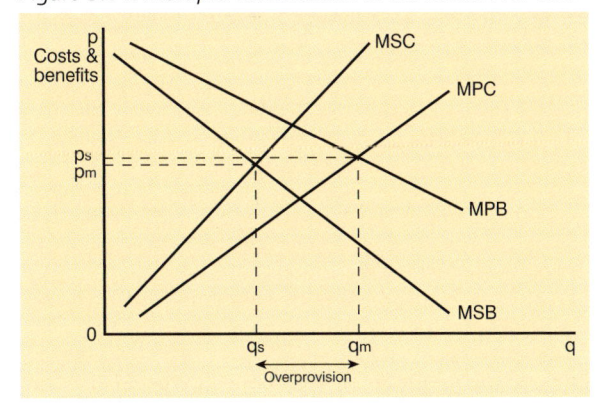

If there is more than one externality to consider, it is important to remember that the free market equilibrium (q_m) is found where MPB = MPC and the socially optimum output is found where MSB = MSC (Figure 9.14). Market failure occurs as Marginal Social Benefit is not equal to Marginal Social Cost at the free market output. Thus cars will tend to be overproduced and overconsumed, as the free market output (q_m) is greater than the socially optimum output.

A useful concept is **net social benefits** i.e. social benefits minus social costs, which takes into account all externalities in consumption and production. If net social benefits are zero, then there is no market failure as social costs must be equal to social benefits. However if net social benefits are positive or negative, then the socially optimum output is not achieved because there is either an underprovision or overprovision of a good or service.

Partial market failure

Externalities are an example of partial market failure. This is because in each of the four types of externalities, the free market allocates resources to enable **some** production or consumption of the good or service which is beneficial to society, however it fails to allocate the correct amount of resources, leading to either under or over provision of the good or service. In other words, whilst a market exists, there is a misallocation of resources.

Externalities and the individual

External costs and benefits are usually discussed with reference to direct impact on third parties. However, some of the external effects of production and consumption can also affect the consumer and producer in the long-run. For example, a smoker damages the health of those around her directly, and also harms her own health which may create the need for expensive treatment (using scarce resources) which may be funded by, for example, the NHS in the future. Similarly, the positive externalities enjoyed by a better-educated workforce can also be of benefit to individuals in the long-run, through increased human capital and higher earning potential.

Summary questions

1. What are external costs? Give three examples not mentioned in this chapter.
2. What are external benefits? Give three examples not mentioned in this chapter.
3. Discuss the merits of using taxes to tackle market failure resulting from the existence of negative externalities.
4. Discuss the merits of using subsidies to tackle market failure resulting from the existence of positive externalities.
5. Using diagrams and with reference to social welfare, show when a ban is justified – and when it is not.
6. Explain how pollution permits can be used to reduce carbon emissions across the globe.
7. When might a government make the consumption of a good compulsory?
8. Why might subsidies prove ineffective at increasing the consumption of a good?
9. Give *two* examples of how regulations can be used to deal with both *positive* externalities and *negative* externalities.
10. "The sale of illegal drugs creates some positive externalities." Evaluate this argument.

Extension questions

A. "All economic activities carry some element of external benefit and cost." Do you agree with this statement? Are there any exceptions?
B. What is the Kyoto protocol? Evaluate its success in reducing global warming.
C. Research what is meant by cost benefit analysis. Consider the private and external costs and benefits resulting from London's hosting of the 2012 Olympics.

Chapter 10
Public, Merit and Demerit Goods

It is hard to imagine a world without government intervention, but this is required when different types of market failure are considered. Have you ever wondered why some goods and services are provided for by the government and not others? The answer lies in the fact that there are '**missing markets**' in which the free market outcome leads to either none of a good or service being produced or what is considered to be the wrong amount.

Private goods

In order to understand public goods, it is necessary to define private goods. These goods have two main characteristics. They are *excludable*, which means that it is possible to prevent other individuals from consuming that good or service. For example, you are able to enjoy eating your own chocolate bar without having to share the benefits with anyone else. Private goods are also *diminishable* or *rivalrous* which means that an individual's consumption of that good reduces the possible consumption for others. Each bite that you take of a chocolate bar reduces the amount available for others to consume. The market mechanism is generally able to allocate private goods efficiently but this is not the case for public goods.

Public goods

Public goods have two characteristics.

1. **Non-excludable** – it is not possible to prevent any other consumer from benefiting from the good or service.

2. **Non-diminishable** or **non-rivalrous** – consumption by one individual does not reduce the amount available for consumption by others.

National defence is an example of a public good. It would be very difficult for one individual to prevent others from protection (non-excludable) and the protection of one person does not reduce the availability of protection for others (non-diminishable).

Public goods and market failure

Figure 10.1: Welfare loss of a public good

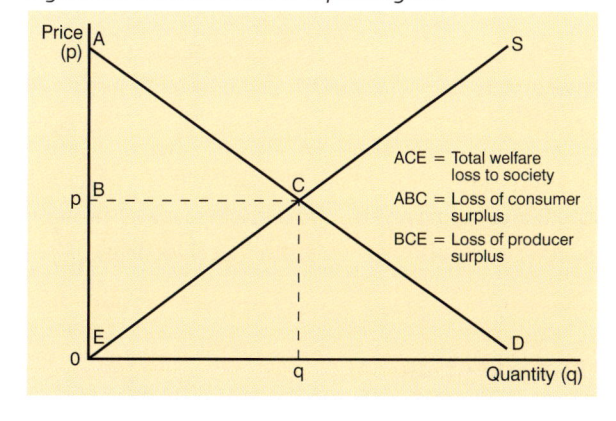

Public goods are a type of market failure which exists because of the *free rider problem*. This is linked to the non excludability characteristic of public goods. If consumers cannot be excluded from benefiting from a good or service, then they have no incentive to pay in the first place. It is assumed that they will 'free ride' as a result, which means benefitting from consumption of a good without paying for it. If all consumers behave in this way, there will be no demand, which gives no incentive for producers to supply the good. The overall effect will be a *missing market* and therefore market failure. The welfare lost in terms of consumer and producer surplus as a result of zero production and consumption in a market is shown in Figure 10.1.

National defence is an example of a public good.

Quasi or Non-pure public goods

These goods have elements of both public and private goods. They are therefore partly provided by the free market. A good example is roads. Roads are a private good in the sense that it is possible to exclude consumers from driving on them, for example the M6 Toll where drivers pay to use the motorway. Roads however have public good elements because they are non diminishable, except during rush hour when there is congestion and one individual's car takes away the use of the road for another. Therefore it can be argued that roads are quasi or non-pure public goods.

Technological change can enable a public good to become a quasi public good as it can change some of its characteristics to that of a private good. Television broadcasting, which was once a public good, has now become excludable so that some viewers are able to pay for additional channels, for example from SKY TV.

Public 'Bads'

Some public goods have negative effects on social welfare and economists add a third characteristic: **non-rejectability**.

For example, pollution caused by a factory or an airport is *non-excludable* (if one local resident is affected, so are others), *non-rivalrous* (disturbance to one resident from noise from a jet taking off does not reduce the amount of noise suffered by others) and also *non-rejectable* (local residents are unable to 'refuse' to consume the pollution).

Public goods and government intervention

The main way in which the government intervenes in the markets for public goods is by direct provision. Since the market fails to provide some goods and services, the government steps in to provide them for its citizens. The production of such goods is financed by general taxation. For example, UK citizens benefit from the government providing national defence in the form of the armed forces and firearms, but are effectively forced to pay for it through taxation.

These goods or services may be produced by nationalised firms which are owned by the government. Alternatively, the government may contract out work to private firms or subsidise firms to give them an incentive to supply public goods. Nationalised firms could be argued to be more allocatively efficient. This is because the government has the ability to ensure that low prices are charged and consumers get more value for their tax money. However these firms may suffer from productive inefficiency as the lack of competition does not give an incentive to drive costs down. The government may therefore decide in some cases that contracting out to competing firms may be more economically efficient. The limitations of direct provision and subsidies are discussed further in Chapter 12.

Education is an example of a merit good.

Merit goods

Examples of merit goods include education, health care and pensions. They have three characteristics.

1. They are associated with **positive externalities** in consumption (see Figure 10.2).

    The external benefits in the case of education would be the benefit to society of a skilled workforce, which is able to compete globally and ultimately increase living standards in a country.

Figure 10.2: Merit goods and positive externalities in consumption

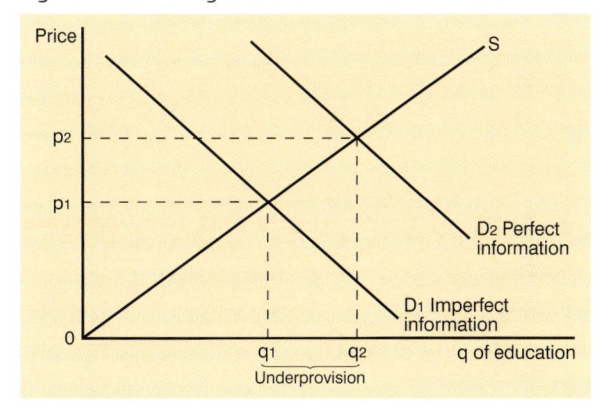

2. The market for a merit good also suffers from **information failure** as consumers do not realise the long run benefits of education at the point of consumption. For example, a pupil's decision to leave formal education at sixteen may be based on a lack of information about the benefits to their future career and income if they continued. Therefore less education is demanded in the free market than would be if full information was available as shown by D1 and D2 in Figure 10.3.

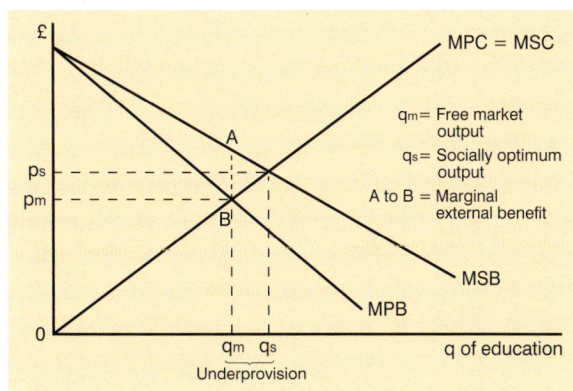

Figure 10.3: Merit goods and information failure

3. Both the association with positive externalities in consumption and information failure lead to the third characteristic, which is the **underprovision** of such a good in the market. Unlike public goods, there is a market for merit goods but the free market does not provide enough of them. This results in an inefficient allocation of resources as the socially optimum output is not achieved. Merit goods are therefore a form of market failure.

69

Demerit goods

Similar to merit goods, demerit goods also have three characteristics. Examples of demerit goods include tobacco, alcohol and junk food.

Figure 10.4: Demerit goods and negative externalities in consumption

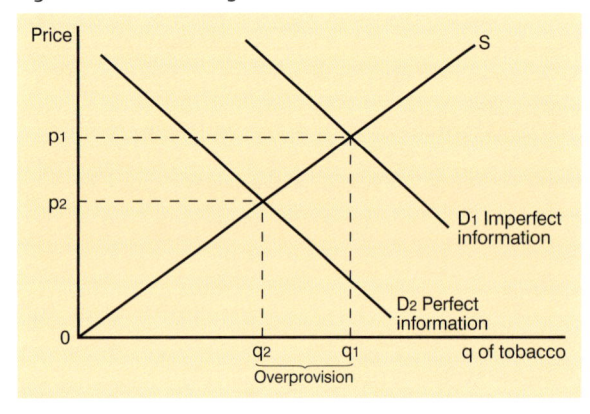

1. They are associated with **negative externalities** in consumption as shown in Figure 10.4.

   The negative externalities in consumption of smoking tobacco are the effects of passive smoking on society and the increased cost of healthcare resulting from smoking-related illness.

2. **Information failure** occurs as consumers do not realise the long run costs at the point of consumption. In the example of smoking, consumers do not consider the long term effects to their health including increasing the risk of cancer. Therefore more cigarettes are demanded in the free market than would be if perfect information was available at the point when smokers light up a cigarette, as shown by D1 and D2 in Figure 10.5.

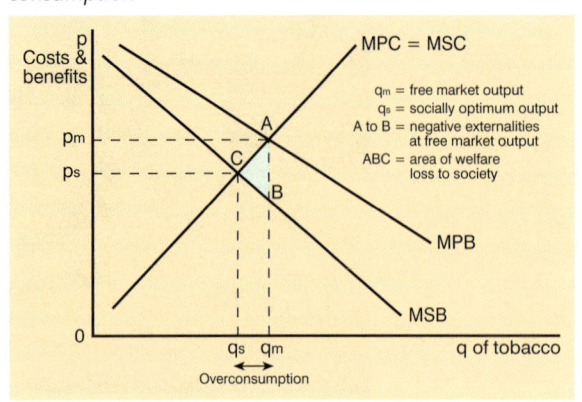

Figure 10.5: Demerit goods and information failure

3. Both of the above characteristics lead to the third, which is the **overprovision** of demerit goods in the market. There is an inefficient allocation of resources as the socially optimum output is not achieved in the free market and therefore market failure occurs.

It should be noted that not all positive or negative externalities in consumption are either merit or demerit goods. Information failure is also required at the point of consumption to be a merit or demerit good.

Signalling function of price

Market failure in the case of merit goods and demerit goods can also be explained in terms of the breakdown of the signalling function of price. Prices carry information about the market with which consumers and producers make their plans. If this information is accurate, then the socially optimum output should be achieved. However, the existence of externalities in consumption and the lack of perfect information at the point of consumption mean that planned supply and demand is based on the inaccurate information carried by the market price. Therefore the equilibrium quantity is likely to be socially undesirable.

Value judgement and the significance of merit goods and demerit goods

The classification of merit goods and demerit goods or the extent to which there is market failure depends on value judgement, or opinion. Putting a numerical value on externalities, for example, is not an easy task and different groups will value them differently, depending on their interests or morals. Governments may also have different views on the significance of merit and demerit goods and the extent of the market failure. Therefore, the type and amount of government intervention may vary significantly between governments and political parties.

Government intervention for merit and demerit goods

There are two main types of government intervention: market-based methods and command and control. Successful government intervention often involves a combination of both methods.

Market-based methods

These are methods which use the price mechanism to change equilibrium price and quantity in the market.

Indirect taxation

As with negative externalities, indirect taxation can be used to correct the overprovision of demerit goods by reducing the quantity in the market and at the same time raise government revenue as can be seen in Figure 10.6. If the tax per unit (B to D) is set so that the new equilibrium achieves the socially optimum output, then the negative externality in consumption is internalised. For example, an indirect tax on alcohol will increase the cost of production for producers which reduces supply to the market (S1 to S2). Consumers are affected by the increase in price from p1 to p2 and the overall quantity of alcohol in the market falls from q1 to q2.

Figure 10.6: Indirect taxation on a demerit good such as alcohol

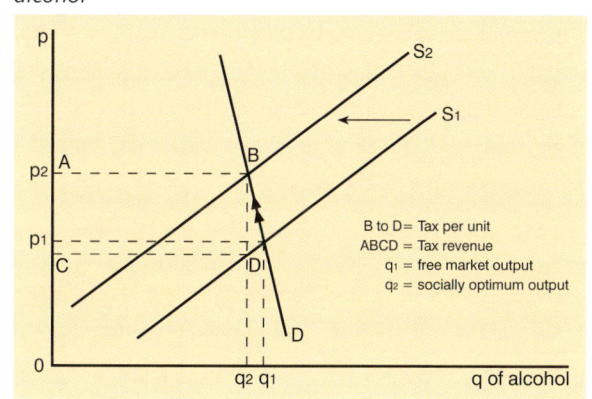

B to D = Tax per unit
ABCD = Tax revenue
q1 = free market output
q2 = socially optimum output

Remember that price elasticity of demand is important to consider. Many demerit goods are addictive in nature and therefore the demand is likely to be price inelastic i.e. not very responsive to changes in price. An increase in price may be ineffective in significantly reducing the quantity of alcohol in the market. However, an indirect tax on a good which has a price inelastic demand will earn the government a lot of revenue (area ABDC). The success of the government intervention is dependent upon the government using the revenue wisely to correct the market failure in additional ways. One option is to use a **hypothecated tax**, which is levied to raise revenue for a specific use, for example the London Congestion Charge raises funds which are dedicated to improving public transport in the city.

Further limitations of indirect taxation are discussed in Chapter 12.

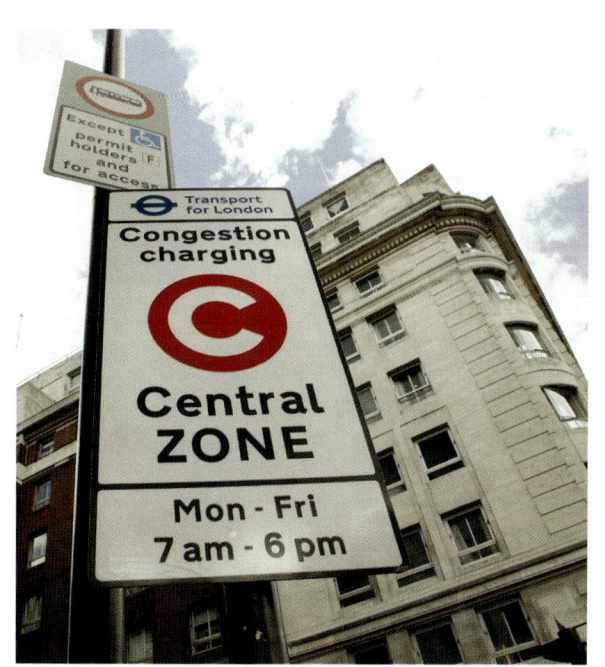

A hypothecated tax is one levied to raise revenue for a specific use such as the London Congestion Charge.

Subsidies

Subsidies are amounts paid by the government to producers for a specific purpose. Subsidies can be used to correct the underprovision of merit goods by increasing the quantity of a good or service in the market. If a subsidy per unit (E to F) is set so

Figure 10.7: Subsidising a merit good

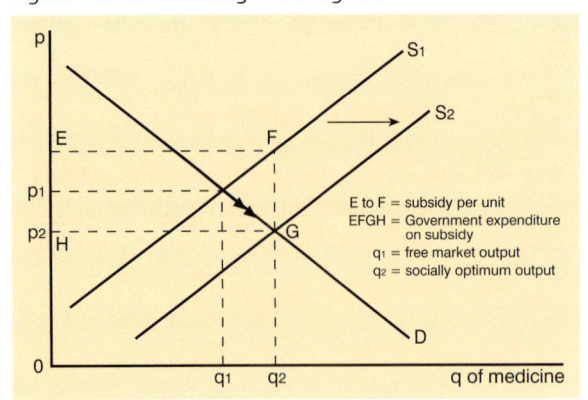

that the new equilibrium achieves the socially optimum output (q2) as shown in Figure 10.7, then the positive externality in consumption is internalised. For example subsidising certain medicines can prevent an unhealthy and unproductive workforce. The subsidy has the effect of decreasing the cost of producing medicine which increases supply to the market (S1 to S2). As a result the price falls from p1 to p2 and the quantity of medicine in the market increases from q1 to q2.

Alternatively, subsidies can be used to encourage consumption of goods which are preferable substitutes to demerit goods (in the government's opinion).

However, subsidies may lead to government failure and further inefficiencies (see Chapter 12). Subsidies cost the government money (area EFGH in Figure 10.7) and therefore result in an opportunity cost i.e. the benefit lost from the government spending money in other areas. If producers do not use the money for what it was intended for or are wasteful with it, then it may not correct the market failure but instead reduce competitiveness and result in productive inefficiency.

Information failure

Whilst information failure is a characteristic of merit and demerit goods, it is also a type of market failure in its own right. It occurs when there are information gaps or asymmetric information between economic agents.

Symmetric information occurs when all economic agents have access to the same information.

Asymmetric information occurs when one or a group of economic agents have more information than other economic agents.

An example of asymmetric information was given by an American economist called George Akerlof. He used the example of second hand cars. When a consumer wants to buy a second hand car, they probably do not know anything about the history of the car. However, the car dealer (producer) will know more about where the car came from and is likely to have more experience in cars generally to know if the second hand car is a peach (a good car) or a lemon (a bad car). There is asymmetric information because the car dealer knows more about the car than the prospective buyer and the buyer has to decide whether or not to trust the information they are given. The car dealer may also hold back information. This means that the car dealer has the upper hand when negotiating a price and market failure may occur because the consumer may end up paying a higher price than the car is actually worth. If the buyer had all the information, they would have paid a lower price.

In economic theory, it is assumed that buyers and sellers have perfect information and resources are allocated accordingly via the price mechanism. However in reality, there may be varying degrees of asymmetric information, which will distort the equilibrium price and therefore lead to a misallocation of resources.

Moral hazard

Moral hazard occurs when individuals are willing to take big risks due the information that they hold. This has been an issue in the insurance market, in which some drivers may drive a lot faster because they know that if they crash the car, the insurance company will pay for the damage. Any market in which there is a bail out for failure can lead to moral hazard.

During the financial crisis of 2007 there was a fear that providing support to banks would encourage greater risk-taking in the future. In a situation where the losses from risk-taking are absorbed by the government, more reckless behaviour than usual may arise.

Command and control methods

Regulation
This involves legislation that enforces more or less consumption of a merit or demerit good respectively.

Examples
Merit good: School is compulsory in the UK and the leaving age was raised in England from 16 to 17 in 2013 and to 18 in 2015.

Demerit good: Smoking was banned in all public places in 2007.

One of the limitations of regulation is that it must be enforced, otherwise consumers will ignore it. This can be costly in terms of administration. There may also be unintended consequences. For example, the banning of smoking in public places may increase litter (a negative externality) from cigarette butts on pavements where individuals are smoking outside instead.

Direct provision
Direct provision is not just applicable to public goods. Some merit goods are provided by the government to ensure there is a socially acceptable amount of a good or service provided. Healthcare and education in the government's view should be available to everyone and not solely to those who can afford it as dictated by the market or those who realise the benefits of it. For example, the National Health Service was set up by the Labour government in the 1940s for this reason. However, in both cases it is still possible to pay for these services if consumers choose to.

Provision of information
The information failure element of merit and demerit goods should not be overlooked as this is one of the reasons why the market fails as a whole. The government can use a variety of methods to ensure that

The government believes that healthcare should be available to everyone and not solely to those who can afford it.

consumers have perfect information at the point of consumption. For example, consumers are much more aware of the dangers of smoking due to warnings on cigarette boxes, education at school, information provided by the NHS and adverts showing the effects of smoking. Banning of advertising on television by tobacco companies has also been enforced in an attempt to reduce smoking.

Summary questions

1. Using examples, explain what is meant by a public good.
2. How do private goods differ from public goods?
3. Explain why pensions are an example of merit goods.
4. Why do demerit goods tend to be overconsumed in a free market?
5. Why might a value judgement be necessary when determining whether a particular good is a merit good or demerit good?
6. Give three examples of how regulation can be used to control the consumption of demerit goods.
7. What is information failure?
8. Give two examples of how information failure can be tackled.
9. Distinguish between market-based and command and control policies.
10. Give three examples from your own experiences of how moral hazard can influence decision-making.

Extension questions

A. To what extent is air a public good?
B. What conflicts may the government face when deciding to intervene in the market for a merit or a demerit good?
C. Evaluate when *direct provision* may be chosen over *subsidies* or *regulation* to increase consumption of a merit good.
D. Research Akerlof's theory of 'peaches' and 'lemons' in the second-hand car market. Use your research to explain the difference between symmetric and asymmetric information, and why this may contribute to market failure.

Chapter 11
Factor Immobility and Inequality

Factor immobility refers to the inability or unwillingness of factors of production (land, labour, capital and enterprise) to be put to their most efficient use. Examples of factor immobility are shown in Table 11.1.

Table 11.1: Examples of factor immobility

Land	Rent control prevents rents rising sufficiently to drive out inefficient businesses from high value sites in a city.
Labour	Family ties deter an unemployed worker from moving to another region where their skills are in demand.
Capital	An insecure or inflexible banking sector fails to provide sufficient affordable funds to allow a business to invest to expand.
Enterprise	Nepotism results in poor management decisions and underperformance in a business.

Flexible factor markets

The efficiency of factor markets is important on both a microeconomic and macroeconomic level. Efficient markets move more quickly towards equilibrium levels of output and price, and this helps the signalling, incentive and rationing functions of price to work more effectively and may also reduce frictional and structural unemployment of not only labour, but also land and capital.

The flexibility of factor markets can be increased through policies such as:

- Reductions in planning restrictions on land use and the regeneration of brown-field and green-field sites
- Retraining of redundant workers
- Development of transferable skills
- Efficient capital and credit markets to provide funding for new business opportunities

Factor immobility

Perhaps the most harmful form of factor immobility is labour immobility: the failure of workers to be willing or able to take advantage of opportunities to find work in the industry in which their human capital is most highly valued.

There are two main causes of labour immobility: geographical and occupational.

Geographical immobility of labour

This refers to the failure of free markets to encourage workers to exchange their human capital for its highest value due to restrictions on physical movement. Typical causes include:

- Family ties to an area
- Cultural ties to an area
- Individual aversion to an area
- Considerable house price differentials (see Figures 11.1 and 11.2 below)
- Language barriers (consider mobility within the EU, for example)
- Residency laws

It is important to note that labour mobility is often severely restricted, on an international level, by immigration laws.

Figure 11.1: Falling demand for labour, falling house prices

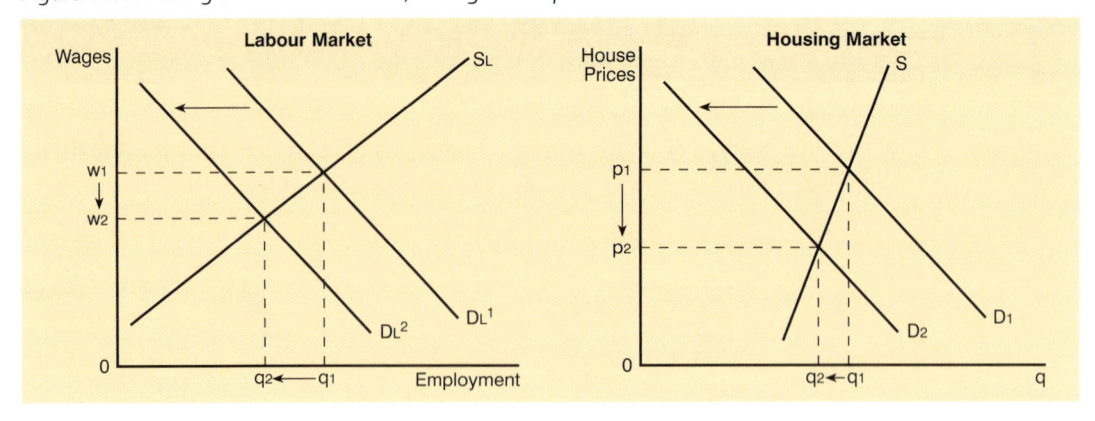

Figure 11.2: Rising demand for labour, rising house prices

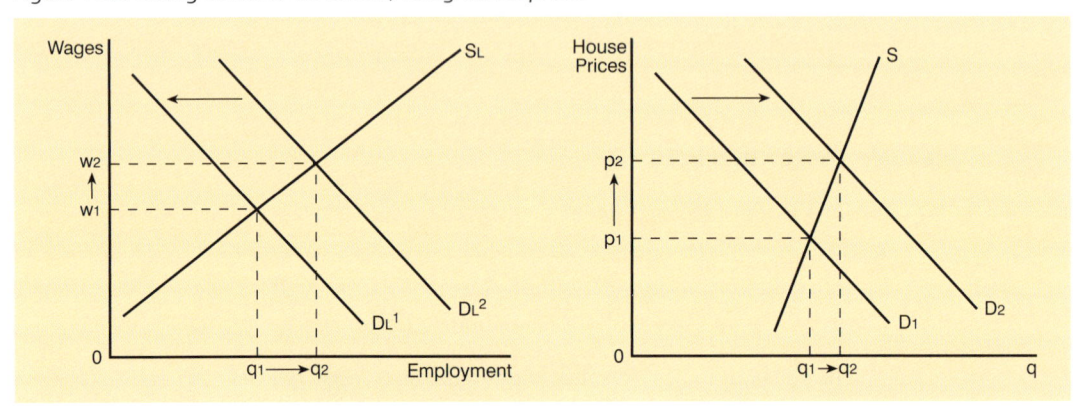

Figure 11.1 represents a labour and housing market in an area with declining job opportunities. This may be due to deindustrialisation or the closure of a major employer in the area. Wages decrease as the demand for workers falls, as do house prices as the average spending power of the local population declines.

Figure 11.2 shows the opposite case. This is a growth area where increasing job opportunities are pushing up average wages and, in turn, leading to a higher demand for housing. But this disparity between house prices can lead to labour immobility, particularly in workers with families and financial commitments. (In general, geographical mobility declines and immobility increases as workers grow older.)

House price differentials contribute significantly to differences in employment rates and earnings differentials across the UK.

The persistence of house price and earnings differentials could be countered by relocation subsidies and allowances (such as the

A 'London Allowance' will help workers to afford accommodation in the capital.

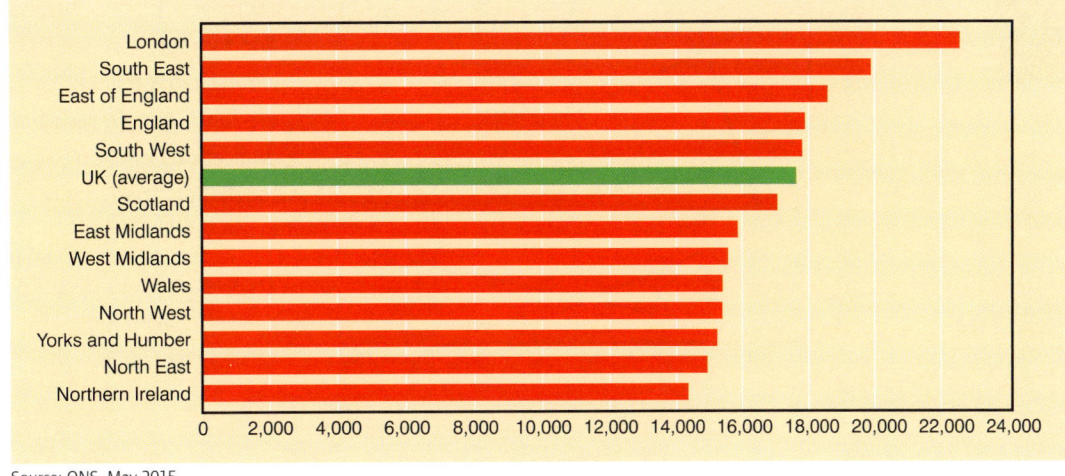

Figure 11.3: Gross domestic household income (£, current prices) by region, 2013

[Bar chart showing gross domestic household income by region in 2013, with values ranging approximately from £14,000 (Northern Ireland) to £22,500 (London). Regions listed top to bottom: London, South East, East of England, England, South West, UK (average), Scotland, East Midlands, West Midlands, Wales, North West, Yorks and Humber, North East, Northern Ireland.]

Source: ONS, May 2015

'London allowance') to help workers take jobs where opportunities are greatest. Figure 11.3 shows how similarly sized areas have substantial differences in household income.

Occupational immobility of labour

This is often linked to geographical immobility due to the tendency for particular industries to be concentrated in certain regions. Occupational immobility is higher when employers undervalue workers' experience in other industries and when there are long periods of apprenticeship and training which restrict entry into a new industry.

Developing transferable skills (general abilities in literacy, numeracy, ICT, people and management skills) is an important way of increasing the human capital of both individuals and the workforce as a whole. As the pattern of production and trade shifts over time, workers and workforces with transferable skills are better able to move out of declining industries (where wages are stagnant or falling) and into growth areas (where wages are rising). In addition to helping individuals to avoid poverty and hardship, this will also lead to lower structural and frictional unemployment in the macroeconomy (see your macroeconomics notes for more detail on these topics!). Retraining policies and welfare to work programmes are important mechanisms for allowing workers to maximise their earnings and productivity.

Inequality and poverty

Inequality is regarded by some economists as a form of market failure, and by others as a cause or effect of market failure.

Poverty can be defined in two ways.

Absolute poverty occurs when an individual is living (or attempting to live) on an income below an accepted minimum level, such as US$1 per day (the measure currently used by the United Nations).

Relative poverty affects the households in the lower percentiles of income in an economy. Relative poverty will always exist wherever there is inequality.

Inequality exists in all economies where workers are rewarded according to their human capital, and where human capital is distributed unevenly between households. Labour is demanded by firms (as a derived demand) in proportion to the extra revenue each worker brings to the firm, and supplied by households according to the wage rate which determines the incentive, or the willingness and ability of each worker, to work. The market mechanism can therefore explain why some workers earn more than others, as shown in Figure 11.4.

Figure 11.4: Wage rate differentials

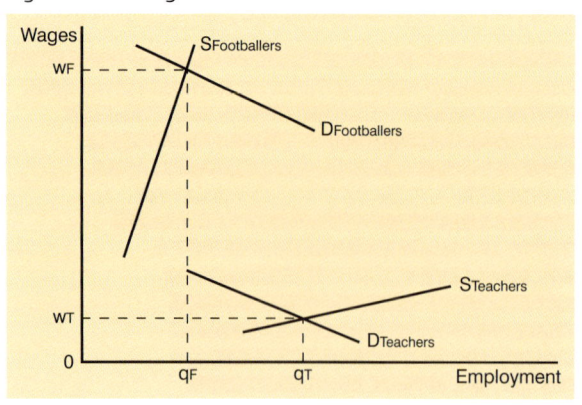

The demand for a worker is higher for footballers than for teachers: a footballer can add far more revenue to their employer each week than a teacher can. In addition, there are fewer people with the natural gifts (and dedication) required to become a professional footballer than there are to become a professional teacher.

Thus fewer footballers are employed – but at a significantly higher wage rate than that earned by teachers.

Inequality and standards of living

For some households, however, the market wage rate may be too low to allow an acceptable standard of living. The National Minimum Wage was discussed in Chapter 6, and other ways the government can attempt to tackle poverty and help households on low (or zero) incomes are:

- Unemployment benefits and welfare to work payments
- Disability and sickness benefits
- Zero price provision or price-capping (e.g. university tuition fees) of merit goods such as healthcare and education
- Subsidised or free transport for certain groups, e.g. pensioners and students
- Direct provision or regulation of key industries such as energy, transport and telecommunications
- Price controls in certain privatised utilities
- Progressive taxation to redistribute income from higher income to lower income households
- Winter fuel allowances for pensioners
- Zero rate VAT for some goods, e.g. children's clothing

The benefits of inequality?

Inequality results from an unequal distribution of human capital. Inequity is the formal term for unfairness, but is it unfair or inequitable that some workers earn more than others?

Some economists argue that some degree of inequality is necessary to provide incentives in the economy. If all school-leavers, regardless of qualifications, attendance record, university aspirations and academic success, knew they would all earn exactly the same wage throughout their career, the incentive to study hard would be much lower than at present. This would reduce productivity for both individuals and the macroeconomy.

Most mixed economies attempt to allow just enough inequality to reward hard work and skills, alongside redistributive fiscal policy and provision of a 'safety net' in the form of the welfare state. One of the main disagreements in political debate is the optimal size of the government, i.e. the ideal level of government intervention in free market economies.

Summary questions

1. What is meant by factor immobility and why does it occur?
2. Why is factor immobility regarded as a source of market failure?
3. Explain, using examples, why geographical and occupational labour immobility may be linked to each other.
4. Why do some regions of the UK have higher levels of GDP per capita than others?
5. What are the main causes of poverty in an economy such as the UK?
6. Evaluate the effectiveness of *three* policies which might be used to tackle poverty in the UK.
7. "Inequality between households is primarily passed down the generations." Why might this be the case and what could be done about this?
8. To what extent should inequality be accepted as a necessary feature of modern economies?
9. Is a welfare state desirable?
10. "Policies on poverty and inequality are a matter for politicians, not economists." To what extent do you agree with this statement?

Extension questions

A. "Wage rate differentials are the main determinant of poverty in the UK." To what extent do you agree with this statement?
B. Research the concept of a 'living wage' and evaluate whether this should replace the minimum wage in the UK.
C. What are the essential features of a society? To what extent must at least some of these be provided by government?
D. "Poverty between nations is of greater concern than poverty within nations." Evaluate this statement, using examples where possible.

Chapter 12
Government Policy and Government Failure

Free markets may lead to market failure, when the allocation of resources is deemed to be inefficient or unfair. Governments can respond to market failure using various policies, which in turn may cause government failure.

Government failure is defined as the negative consequences of a policy response to market failure. This negative impact may be less than, equal to, or even greater than the negative consequences of the initial market failure.

Causes of government failure

Government failure arises for a number of reasons, including:

1. Imperfect or inadequate information
Data can be inaccurate due to time lags, errors in recording or errors in reporting. This creates difficulties when choosing the right policy and setting the correct level of response.

2. Law of unintended consequences
Government policy rarely avoids side-effects, some of which may be beneficial but some of which may be harmful. For example, tightening enforcement of under-age drinking laws by raiding pubs more frequently and fining landlords may reduce alcohol problems in pubs, but may lead to more illegal drinking in parks or on the streets.

Figure 12.1: Opportunity costs of education and healthcare provision

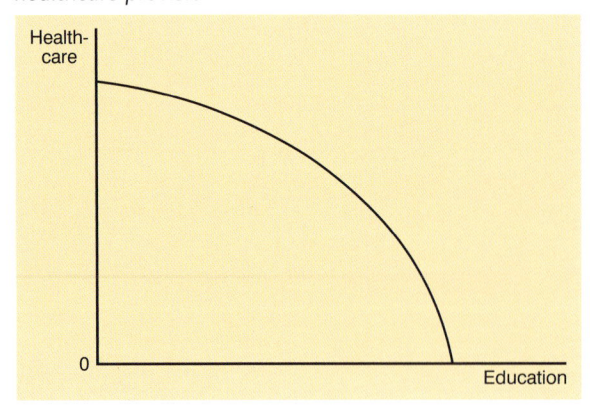

3. Opportunity costs and administration costs
The central economic problem is one of scarcity and the scarcity of government resources is a key issue when deciding how to allocate budgets to tackle market failure. Prisons keep offenders locked away but the financial cost and opportunity cost of the prison system is high. Similarly, improving education facilities can only be achieved by not improving, say, healthcare.

4. Public choice theory
Economic policies are generally implemented by politicians, who in a democracy must periodically seek re-election. This can create problems such as **short-termism**, where politicians tackle the most pressing or popular problems first. This may lead to underfunding of less fashionable issues (adequate investment in transport infrastructure, or the pensions crisis, for example) and create long-run government failure which future governments may then have to take more drastic action to resolve. In addition, politicians may also be open to lobbying from special interest groups and in extreme cases **corruption** may cause sub-optimal decisions to be made. With regard to the regulation of certain industries, **regulatory capture** occurs when the government body which oversees regulatory standards has vested interests in the industry they are monitoring.

5. Conflicting objectives

Microeconomic policies may have macroeconomic consequences. For example, increasing taxes on petrol or imposing tighter regulation on smoking and drinking may affect sectors such as the leisure and travel industries and lead to unemployment if the price inelasticity of these goods leads to lower spending in other areas.

Government policies and government failure

Revision note: the various policies available to correct market failure can be divided into two categories, **market-based** and **command and control**.

Market-based policies

Figure 12.2: Internalising a negative externality

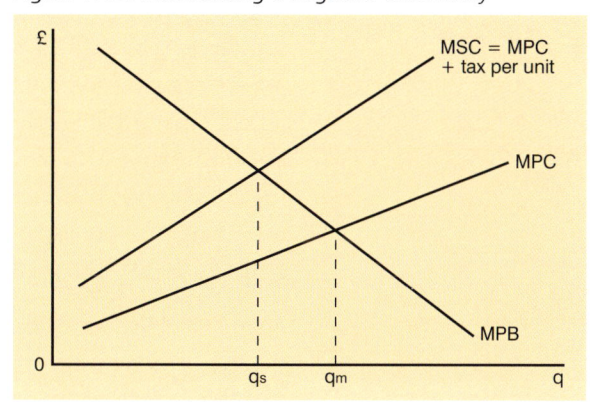

Figure 12.3: Welfare loss and underestimating external costs

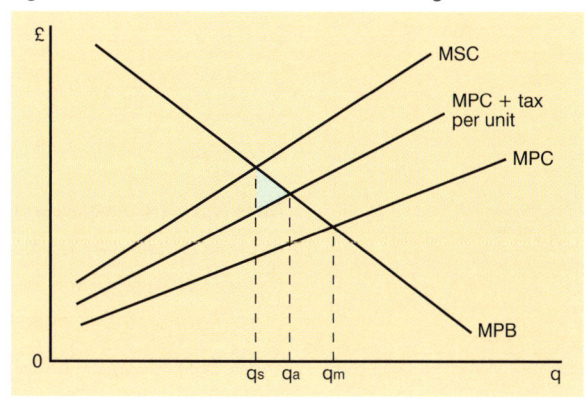

Figure 12.4: Welfare loss and overestimating external costs

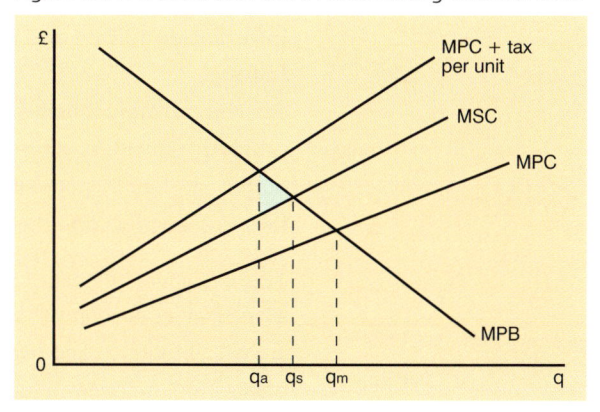

Market-based methods aim to shift the equilibrium price and output towards more socially desirable levels using the market mechanism. The main policies are taxes and subsidies and removing information failure.

Taxes and government failure

Figure 12.2 shows a market where the imposition of an indirect tax has been used to internalise a negative externality; marginal social costs are now equal to marginal private costs plus the tax per unit, and the socially optimal output level has been achieved.

However, this policy only works this well when the external cost per unit (i.e. the extent to which marginal social costs diverge from marginal private costs) can be exactly calculated.

Figures 12.3 and 12.4 show markets where the imposition of an environmental tax has underestimated and overestimated external costs respectively.

On both diagrams, the welfare loss resulting from the incorrect level of tax is shown by the shaded area.

Another problem associated with taxes on harmful or demerit goods is when the consumption of these goods forms a higher proportion of spending in lower income households than in higher income households. This is usually true for cigarettes and alcohol and such a tax may therefore be regressive and lead to increased inequality.

Higher levels of taxation in the economy can also have a disincentive effect in two key areas: the incentive of labour to work and the incentive of entrepreneurs to engage in business activity.

Subsidies and government failure

Subsidising the supply of goods with positive externalities, merit goods and public goods can be seen as a simple method of increasing the provision of goods which would otherwise be partially or totally under-provided.

The main problem resulting from subsidies is the **opportunity cost** of government funding, which could have been used in other areas. This is of particular concern when the allocation of resources may be influenced by political factors and Public Choice Theory suggests that, in this case, suboptimal outcomes may occur.

Figure 12.5: Welfare loss and underestimating external benefits

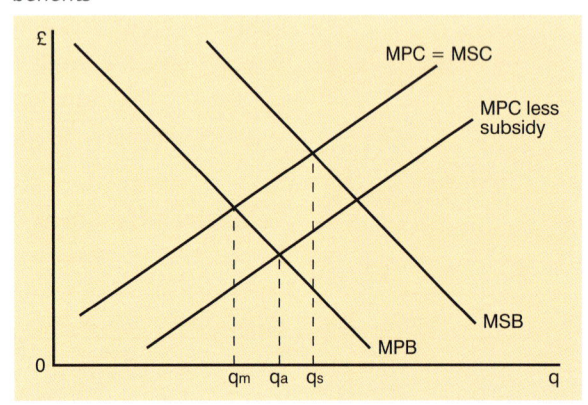

Figure 12.6: Welfare loss and overestimating external benefits

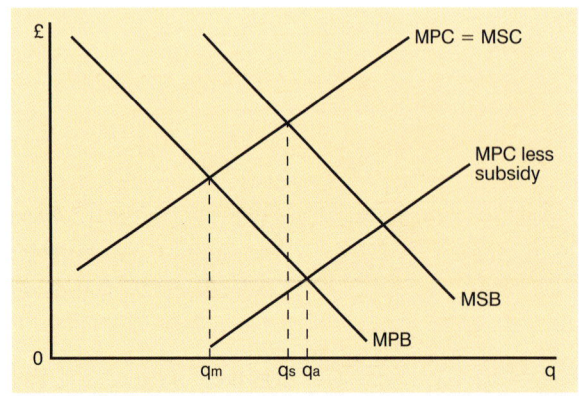

Figure 12.7: Over-production and over-consumption of video games

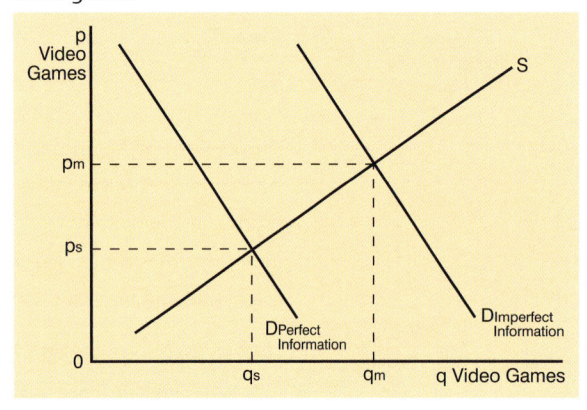

In addition, the subsidy must be set at the correct level to achieve a socially desirable output. Figure 12.5 shows a market where the subsidy is too small to decrease marginal private costs sufficiently to increase actual output (q_a) to the socially optimal output level (q_s). Figure 12.6 shows a market where the subsidy was too generous and actual output (q_a) is now higher than that which would be socially optimal (q_s).

Another problem with subsidising provision is the lack of, or reduction in **profit motive**. A subsidised producer may allow other costs to rise (productive inefficiency), fail to produce enough of the good to a sufficiently high standard (allocative inefficiency) or fail to innovate (dynamic inefficiency) as government funding protects the organisation from free market forces.

Note also that partially subsidising the supply of public goods may not be successful as, due to the non-rivalry and non-excludability of these goods, it is extremely difficult for the supplier to collect revenue from all users. A more drastic action may be required, such as total provision by the government (see below).

Information failure and government failure

Whereas taxes and subsidies aim to manipulate supply to create a (more) socially-optimal output level, policies to address information failures are designed to change demand.

To use a simple example, it may be the case in a free market economy that computer games are over-produced and over-consumed, and books are under-produced and under-

Figure 12.8: Under-production and under-consumption of books

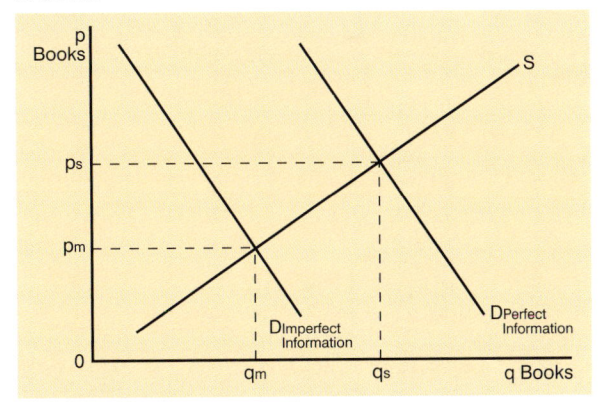

consumed. This may be due to a lack of clear information regarding the benefits provided by reading books, and the costs incurred by computer games. This situation is shown in Figures 12.7 and 12.8, where actual demand is shown as D_{Imperfect information} in both cases, and the socially optimal level of demand as D_{Perfect information}.

This market failure can be resolved by addressing the information failure. Public information campaigns could, in theory, shift the demand for computer games inwards and shift the demand for books outwards, moving both markets towards the level of demand which would arise if there was perfect information. However, this may not occur. If neither demand curve moves as a result of the information campaign this is a case of opportunity cost: the same outcome would have arisen from no intervention, and the funds could have been used more effectively elsewhere. It is even possible that government campaigns have the opposite effect to that desired by actually increasing the attractiveness of demerit goods and reducing demand for merit goods. UK drugs education has changed in recent years from a 'Just Say No' stance to one of providing greater information on the risks of drug-taking, but some critics have argued that any perceived loosening of policy or apparent endorsement of drug use may actually increase demand, despite aiming to decrease use. Similarly, recent changes to opening hours of pubs in England were designed to reduce alcohol consumption – by apparently removing the need to binge-drink – but the success of this policy is seriously under doubt, perhaps with consumption actually increasing in line with the drinking time available.

Command and control policies

Command and control measures remove or restrict the operation of free markets. Typical measures include bans, direct provision and regulation.

Bans and government failure
Banning a good is only usually socially desirable (and justifiable) when social costs exceed social benefits at all levels of output (see Figure 8.3 in Chapter 8). Banning in any other situation will lead to welfare loss.

In addition, banning rather than taxing a good removes the possibility of raising revenue. Obviously, this argument only holds when the socially optimal level of output is greater than zero, and thus a total ban is not justified anyway.

Direct provision and government failure
As with subsidies, direct provision by the government creates opportunity costs. In the case of major industries such as healthcare, education and transport, huge costs are incurred by the government in funding and maintaining large capital projects and paying extensive wage bills (for example, the NHS is the largest employer in the UK).

Critics of direct provision highlight the **inefficiencies** of not-for-profit organisations. Without the profit motive to ensure that revenues are maximised and costs minimised, it is argued that resources will be wasted and, over time, there is little incentive for service to improve. However, the provision of merit goods must take into account the social benefits as well as the private benefits and costs. Vaccinating children against certain illnesses creates positive externalities well into the future. In addition, the value of a human life (let alone different qualities of life) and the value of education is very difficult to calculate (and, for some individuals, to take a long-run view on) and it may be decided by the government that providing some

The government could set a maximum price for energy.

goods at zero price to all who want them is the socially-optimal outcome. It should be noted that even within the government there will be opportunity costs and even unintended consequences at play. For example, a decision to reduce funding for cleaning in a hospital to increase nurse-to-patient ratios may result in falling hygiene levels and, perhaps, lead to problems such as superbugs.

Regulation and government failure

Regulation is used to monitor and control industries which have considerable monopoly power. It is unlikely that all monopoly industries are regulated to the same degree, mainly because of the administrative costs of funding regulatory bodies to oversee competition. In the UK, it is mainly monopoly suppliers of strategic or essential goods, and natural monopolies, which are regulated closely.

The main problems associated with regulation are regulatory capture and unintended consequences.

Regulatory capture may arise when the regulatory body shares some of the interests of the industry being regulated. This may occur because the best people to regulate an industry are those who have worked in that sector and understand its issues. However, the regulators may have friends (or even shares!) in the sector and this could, according to Public Choice Theory, influence their decisions. There may also be a psychological aspect to regulatory capture, whereby familiarity with an industry and the individuals controlling it leads to a build up of implicit support, which limits the impartiality of its regulation.

Unintended consequences result from the implementation of a policy which, in this context, aims to increase provision of a good or reduce its price, but which has other side-effects. For example, limiting the ability of gas suppliers to raise prices to customers may make them less willing to supply houses and businesses in isolated locations. This could lead to the regulator insisting on guaranteed supply to all properties in the country, which may lead to the company raising the price of boiler maintenance, for example.

Regulation of industries which supply demerit goods is a common way of restricting both demand and supply. For example, alcohol can only be sold in certain outlets at certain times to customers of a certain age. However, such regulation may simply not work. Underage drinking and after-hours opening are common features of UK drinking culture and, again, opportunity cost is perhaps an issue here. It may be the case that the perceived costs resulting from these activities is deemed to be lower than the costs of enforcing existing legislation. Critics of such an approach would stress the possible long-run implications of the government 'turning a blind eye' to, for example, teenage drinking. Public Choice conspiracists would perhaps argue that the government does not wish to lose potential voters!

Maximum and minimum prices

The government may intervene in a market where it decides the equilibrium price is too high or too low. Typically, a maximum price is set where the price of a necessity is deemed too high (thus causing inequality and/or poverty) and a minimum price is set where the price of a good (or the price of a factor of production, such as wage rates in some industries) is deemed too low for its supplier to enjoy a satisfactory standard of living.

The price of two very important commodities rose rapidly in 2008: energy and food. In an instance such as this it is possible that a government decides that the market is too high and sets a maximum level, as shown in Figure 12.9.

Figure 12.9: Impact of a maximum price

The maximum price p_{max} increases the willingness and ability of consumers to demand the good, and quantity demanded rises from the equilibrium level of q_1 to q_2. However, at price p_{max} the willingness and ability of producers to supply the good falls to q_3. The maximum price therefore causes excess demand, or a shortage of ($q_2 - q_3$) and thus a policy designed to make a good more affordable actually reduces the quantity available.

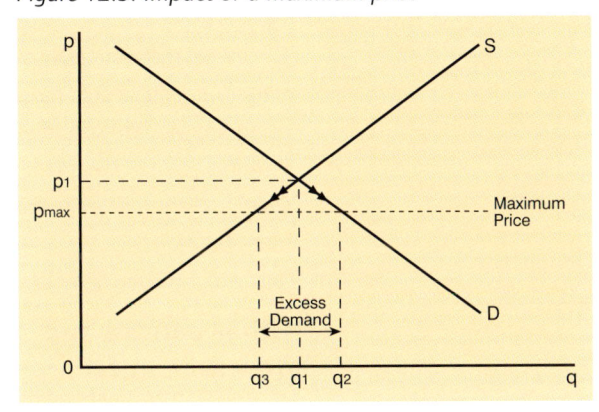

Figure 12.10: Shadow markets and maximum prices

In addition to causing shortages, it is possible that unscrupulous suppliers could sell their output in a shadow market and actually make the good even more unaffordable than before government intervention.

If output q_3 can be sold informally it can raise price to p_2 (read across from the demand curve at this output level), which is above both the maximum price and the market equilibrium. In the long-run, however, it could be argued that this higher price would attract suppliers into the (shadow) market and supply would increase in line with the greater incentive of the higher price.

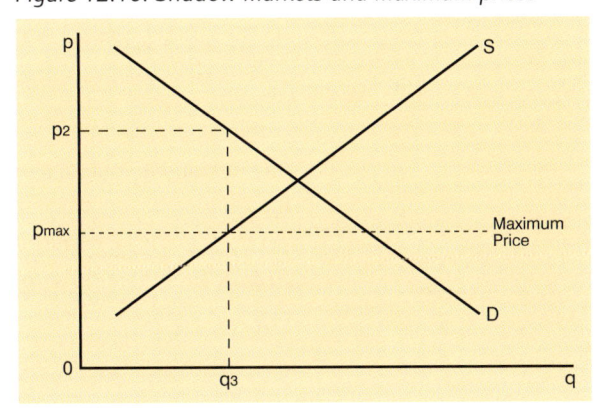

Figure 12.11: Impact of a minimum price

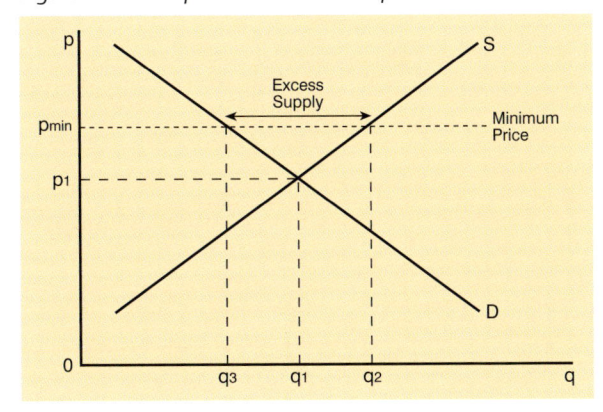

Finally, it is important to note that the maximum price must be set below the market equilibrium – otherwise it will have no effect at all!

A minimum price may also lead to disequilibrium. Figure 12.11 shows a market where the minimum price p_{min} has been imposed to support earnings of suppliers of this good.

However, although the minimum price (also known as price support) increases the willingness and ability of producers to supply the good (quantity supplied rises from the equilibrium level of q1 to q2) consumers are less willing and able to purchase at the higher price and there will be excess supply, or a glut, of (q2 − q3).

Note, also, that a minimum price is only effective where it is set above the market equilibrium.

Maximum and minimum prices in combination with other measures

It could be argued that the problems of disequilibrium created by enforcing non-market prices on both buyers and sellers could be resolved by subsidising production in conjunction with a maximum price and subsidising demand (perhaps through a voucher scheme) in conjunction with a minimum price.

Figure 12.12: Maximum price and subsidised supply

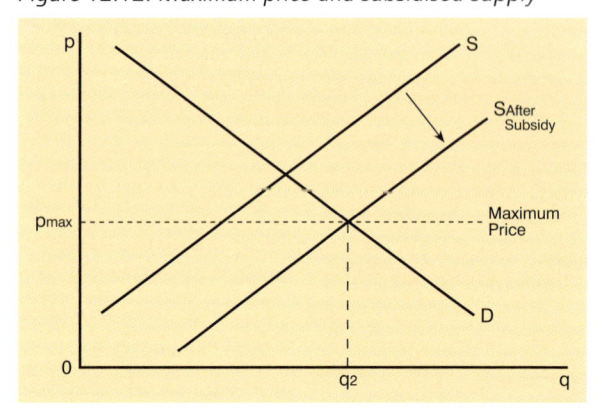

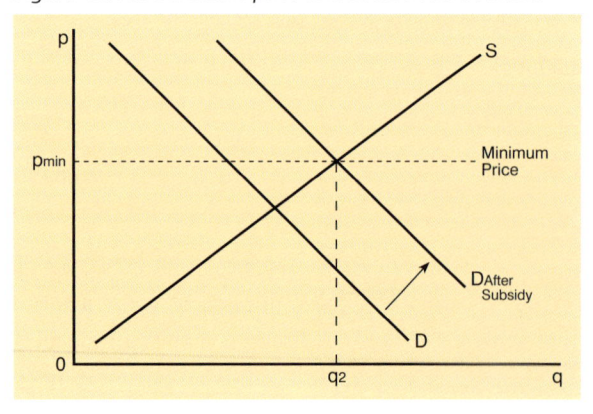

Together, the policies create equilibria at the desired price and output levels, as shown on Figures 12.12 and 12.13.

Of course, the more astute of you will see that these outcomes could have been achieved by using appropriate subsidies in the first place! Perhaps more complex policy responses simply create greater possibilities for government failure?

Figure 12.13: Minimum price and subsidised demand

Other policies and government failure

Some policies have already been critiqued in some detail in earlier chapters, including buffer stock schemes in Chapter 6 and cap and trade emissions policies in Chapter 8.

It should also be noted that a combination of market-based and command and control measures may be necessary in some cases where the damage caused to social welfare from market failure is seen as particularly high.

Summary questions

1. Distinguish carefully, using an example of each, between market failure, government policy and government failure.

2. Explain one financial cost and one opportunity cost associated with increasing the provision of library services.

3. Consider the problem of refuse disposal in the UK. Explain three possible ways of increasing recycling and reducing waste, and then outline possible government failures which could result from each.

4. Why may public sector organisations be inefficient? What could be done to limit government failures associated with regulation and direct provision?

5. Copy Figures 12.9 and 12.10 and show the impact on consumer and producer surplus of government intervention (a) without a shadow market, and (b) with a shadow market.

6. In which industries might a *minimum* price be desirable? Explain why.

7. In which industries might a *maximum* price be desirable? Explain why.

8. What policies could be used to reduce the consumption of unhealthy food? Consider the forms of government policy which might arise for each policy.

9. "All governments are constrained by Public Choice Theory." To what extent do you agree with this statement?

10. "Despite government failure, governments are still essential." To what extent do you agree?

Extension questions

A. Is it possible to draw Figures 12.3, 12.4, 12.5 and 12.6 in such a way as to create a greater welfare loss *after* government intervention than the loss under free market conditions?

B. Research the regulatory bodies existing in the UK at present. Which types of industry are they used to oversee? Why do you think this is the case?

C. Can you think of a government policy for which the market failure it eradicates is far greater than any government failure it may incur?

D. Should governments always try to reduce monopoly power?

Index

Absolute poverty 77
Ad valorem tax 14
Adam Smith 7, 18
Agricultural markets 44
Allocative efficiency 5, 50, 82
Allocative function of price 17
Allocative inefficiency 52
Anti-competitive practices 49
Asymmetric information 72
Average costs 50

Bans 60
Bans and government failure 83
Barriers to entry 49
Behavioural economics 6
Brand loyalty 49
Bureaucracy and compliance costs 54

Cap and trade/pollution permit trading 62-3
Capital 75
Collusion 52
Collusive agreements 55
Command and control methods 73-4
Command and control policies 83-5
Command economies 46
Commodities markets 42-3
Competition and Markets Authority (CMA) 55
Competitive demand 30, 33
Competitive supply 35
Complements 10, 30
Composite demand 34-5
Composite supply 35
Compulsory consumption 61
Concentration 51
Consumer surplus 19-20, 22
Corruption 80
Costs of production 13
Cross price elasticity of demand 30

Demand curve 9
Demand theory 9-11
Demerit goods 70-4
Derived demand 34
Diminishing marginal utility 9
Direct provision and government failure 83
Diseconomies of scale 54
Disequilibrium 17, 19
Disutility 10
Division of labour 7
Dominant position abuse 55
Dynamic efficiency 53, 82

Economic goods 5
Economic regulators 55
Economies of scale 53
Elasticity 23-32
Enterprise 75
External benefits 56
External costs 56
Externalities 58-66

Factor immobility 75-7
Factor substitutability 32
Financial economies of scale 53
Financial markets 43-4
Flexible factor markets 75
Free goods 5
Free market economies 46

Geographical immobility of labour 75
Government policy and government failure 80-6

Homogenous products 49
Housing market 41-2
Hypothecated tax 71

Immigration 40
Imperfect information 80
Incentive function of price 17
Income 10
Income elasticity of demand 28
Indirect taxation 13, 71
Inefficiencies 83
Inequality and poverty 77-8
Inequality and standards of living 78
Information failure 69-70, 72
Information failure and government failure 82-3
Invisible hand 18
Irrational behaviour 6

Joint demand 30, 33-34
Joint supply 35

Labour 75
Labour demand 36-7
Labour market 36
Labour supply 36
Land 75
Law of diminishing returns 12
Law of unintended consequences 88
Long run 51
Luxuries 29

Management costs 54
Managerial economies of scale 53
Marginal external benefits 59
Marginal external costs 59
Marginal private benefits 59
Marginal private costs 59
Marginal social benefits 59
Marginal social costs 59
Market failure 1, 46-8
Market investigations 55
Markets 1
Markets and equilibrium 16-22
Maximising behaviour 5
Maximum and minimum prices 85-6
Merger control 55
Merit goods 69, 70-4
Minimum wage 40-1
Missing markets 67
Mixed economies 46
Monopoly 49
Monopsony 45
Moral hazard 72
Motivation 54

Nationalisation 55
Natural monopolies 54
Necessities 29
Net social benefit 56, 65
New technology 13
Non-rejectability 68

Occupational immobility of labour 77
Oligopoly 52
Opportunity cost 2, 3, 80, 82
Overprovision 70

Partial market failure 65-6
Perfect and imperfect competition 49-51
Personal carbon allowances 63
Point elasticity 24
Positive externalities 69
Price controls 56

Price elasticity of demand 23-4
Price elasticity of demand and indirect taxation 26-7
Price elasticity of demand and total revenue 25-6
Price elasticity of supply 31-2
Price makers 49, 50
Price takers 12
Price wars 52
Private benefits 56
Private costs 56
Private goods 67
Privatisation 55
Producer cartels 14
Producer surplus 20-2
Production possibility frontier 3-4, 50
Productive efficiency 5, 82
Productive inefficiency 52
Profit 12
Profit maximisation 6
Profit motive 82
Property rights extension 61-2
Public 'bads' 68
Public choice theory 80
Public goods 67-8
Public goods and market failure 67
Purchasing economies of scale 53

Quasi or non-pure public goods 68

Rational behaviour 6
Rationing function of price 17
Real wage rate 38
Regulation 61
Regulation and government failure 84
Regulation limits 55
Regulatory capture 80, 84
Relative poverty 78
Road pricing 63

Scarce resources 1
Short-run 51
Short-termism 80
Signalling function of price 17, 70
Social benefits 56
Social costs 56
Social science 6
Social welfare maximisation 6
Spare capacity 31
Specialisation 7-8
Subsidies 14, 27-8, 61, 65
Subsidies and government failure 82
Substitutes 10, 30
Superior goods 29
Supply theory 12-15
Symmetric information 72

Tastes 11
Tax and benefit system 38
Taxation 56
Taxes 60
Taxes and government failure 81-2
Technical economies of scale 53-4
Total revenue 12, 25

Underprovision 69
Unintended consequences 84

Value judgements 4

Wage elasticity of demand 38-9
Wage elasticity of supply 38-9
Wages 6
Wealth 10